One Perfect Day

One Perfect Day

the selling of the american wedding

Rebecca Mead

THE PENGUIN PRESS

New York

2007

THE PENGUIN PRESS
Published by the Penguin Group
Penguin Group (USA) Inc., 375 Hudson Street, New York, New York 10014, U.S.A.
Penguin Group (Canada), 90 Eglinton Avenue East, Suite 700, Toronto, Ontario,
Canada M4P 2Y3 (a division of Pearson Penguin Canada Inc.) • Penguin Books Ltd,
80 Strand, London WC2R 0RL, England • Penguin Ireland, 25 St. Stephen's Green,
Dublin 2, Ireland (a division of Penguin Books Ltd) • Penguin Books Australia Ltd,
250 Camberwell Road, Camberwell, Victoria 3124, Australia (a division of Pearson
Australia Group Pty Ltd) • Penguin Books India Pvt Ltd, 11 Community Centre,
Panchsheel Park, New Delhi – 110 017, India • Penguin Group (NZ), Cnr Airborne
and Rosedale Roads, Albany, Auckland 1310, New Zealand (a division of Pearson
New Zealand Ltd) • Penguin Books (South Africa) (Pty) Ltd, 24 Sturdee Avenue,
Rosebank, Johannesburg 2196, South Africa

Penguin Books Ltd, Registered Offices:
80 Strand, London WC2R 0RL, England

First published in 2007 by The Penguin Press,
a member of Penguin Group (USA) Inc.

ISBN 978-1-59420-088-5

Printed in the United States of America
1   3   5   7   9   10   8   6   4   2

Designed by Claire Vaccaro and Amanda Dewey

for George

Contents

One Perfect Day

Preface

In the early years of this century a new word, and a new stereotype, entered the public discourse: the Bridezilla. The creature characterized by this disparaging term was immediately recognizable. She was a young woman who, upon becoming engaged, had been transformed from a person of reason and moderation into a self-absorbed monster, obsessed with her plans to stage the perfect wedding, an event of spectacular production values and flawless execution, with herself as the star of the show. In her quest to pull off this goal she was blithely willing to wreck friendships, offend parents, harass caterers well past the point of patience, and burn through money more rapidly than a fire consumes forest in a dry August.

The alleged phenomenon of the Bridezilla spawned numerous newspaper articles that recounted her exploits with gleeful censure. The *New York Times* told of one bride who had demanded that her attendants all color their hair the same shade of blond; another who had procured a swatch of the purple wallpaper from the hotel suite in which she would be spending her wedding night so that her florist could find blooms that were an exact match; and another who insisted, before a barefoot beach wedding, that her husband's groomsmen all endure a pedicure. The horrors of encountering a Bridezilla, or worse, unwittingly becoming one, were such that Carley Roney, the cofounder of the online wedding-planning company The Knot, was asked on CNN how a woman might know when she had crossed the line into Bridezilla territory: "You forget that your friends have lives, that people might not be able to come to your seventeen fittings," she said.

The phenomenon moved into other media. A "Bridezilla" book was published with the subtitle "True Tales from Etiquette Hell," featuring on its cover an alarmingly oversized cartoon bride clutching, in one hand, a diminutive, frantic groom, with a tiny bridesmaid in a vile yellow dress in the other. Inevitably, there was a reality television show: In its first season *Bridezillas* followed the wedding preparations of nine overwrought and hysterical brides, one of whom was so concerned that her dress remain unwrinkled and her makeup unsmudged that she refused to let her new husband near her all night. And equally inevitably, newspaper reporters identified the so-called Groomzilla: the husband-to-be who becomes obsessed with the typeface on the invitations and undergoes a regimen of eyebrow waxing and facial microdermabrasion in advance of his big day.

The idea of the Bridezilla gained common currency, and it was easy to understand why. Just about everyone knows someone, or knows of someone, whose wedding plans have taken on the proportions of a military operation, whose wedding costs have ballooned beyond economic prudence, and whose attention to wedding-day production values would put a Broadway set designer to shame. The term was applicable to brides whose resources permitted the casting aside of a three-thousand-dollar wedding dress a week before the ceremony in favor of an alternative model, as well as to those budget brides who spent every evening scouring eBay for cut-price wedding favors or who prided themselves on hand-threading ribbon into 150 wedding-information booklets for their guests.

But it seemed to me, as I witnessed the urgency with which the Bridezilla term was embraced, that there was more to the phenomenon than the identification of a particularly unpleasant breed of bride. When a stereotype is so swiftly absorbed into the popular culture it is a sure sign that something larger is at stake; and what appeared to me to be expressed in the vilification of the Bridezilla was a much wider ambivalence among the general public over the direction weddings in America were taking. Blaming the bride, while making for colorful feature stories and cruelly riveting television programming, wasn't an adequate explanation for what seemed to be underlying the concept of the Bridezilla: that weddings themselves were out of control, and that a sense of proportion had been lost, not just individually but in the culture at large.

This isn't to suggest that people all over the country were wringing their hands at the weddings they attended—though those who were could probably be found everywhere. The majority, though, were throwing up those hands in puzzled bemusement or, at the most, dumbfounded exasperation, while at the same time throwing themselves wholeheartedly into the increasingly elaborate celebrations to which they had been invited. ("When did the softball game become part of a wedding?" one older acquaintance asked me, having recently married off two daughters in weekend-long festivities and found himself swinging a bat on both occasions.) No one wants to find fault with anything so cheering, and so emotionally significant, as a wedding. But at the same time, weddings often prompt a sense of disquiet—all this, just for one day?—among the guests, and, when they will admit it, the couple at the altar. So the pillorying of the Bridezilla figure (who has come to seem to me hardly less fictional than her Japanese monster ancestor, Godzilla) provides a way to separate off, into safe quarantine, the disconcerting sense that the way we conduct weddings has somehow gone wrong; that priorities have changed, and purpose has gone awry. The Bridezilla caricature is a stand-in representing a much larger anxiety: that we are all living in a Bridezilla culture.

How did this happen? What are the forces that are contributing to this increase in wedding pressure, not just among so-called Bridezillas, but among all American brides and grooms? And what is the significance—beyond the impact on the purses and personalities of marrying couples, their friends, and their families—of the escalation of the American wedding? What, in other words, does the American wedding tell us about the rest of American life? It was questions such as these that propelled the writing of this book, as well as a hunch that some answers might be found not by looking at the grotesque behavior of a handful of individuals, from whose excesses an amusing but ultimately trivial tale might be wrought, but by looking at the larger context—at the wedding culture in which those individuals are immersed.

If the state of the American wedding strikes the bride, groom, family member, and guest as troubled (as appeared to me to be the case while researching and writing this book, given the way in which almost everyone to whom I mentioned its subject immediately rolled his or her eyes in recognition, and then insisted on telling me about a niece's, or sister's, or best friend's wedding plans gone wild), then who, I wondered, was happy about the way in which Americans were getting married? In whose interest is it that weddings should be this way? Who, or what, begat Bridezilla?

In order to seek an answer to this question, I decided to turn my attention from weddings themselves—the finished productions upon which so much effort has been lavished—and to focus on the less examined side of weddings:

what has come to be called the wedding industry. This term is used as a catch-all expression to describe the infrastructure of service providers and businesses, ranging from individual entrepreneurs to massive corporations, that seek to provide the bride and groom with the accoutrements of the wedding day—and, in many cases, seek to do business with them long after the wedding day is over. It is a capacious category, one that encompasses the small-town florist supplying bridal bouquets and boutonnieres as well as department-store conglomerates that compete for bridal-registry business. The expression also refers to the wedding media—the magazines and Web sites and television shows that court the bridal customer, or simply appeal to the apparently limitless appetite among Americans at large for coverage of celebrity weddings (in publications such as *InStyle* magazine) and for insight into the wedding dramas of real people, such as those whose plans are chronicled by the hugely popular Learning Channel show *A Wedding Story*.

Weddings in America have long been identified by commercial interests as offering a likely prospect: In the spring of 1901, a trade journal for storekeepers called the *Dry Goods Economist* published a jauntily written item entitled, "June Brides a Fair Mark," which advised, "The merchant of refinement may reach all or nearly all, and tell in an unobtrusive way of how much you can do for them in the taking care of many details incidental to the preparation of a wedding trousseau." Social historians date the establishment of what we would now recognize as a wedding industry as having occurred between the 1920s and 1950s, as jewelers, gown manufacturers, and caterers set standards to which American brides were encouraged, through the bridal media, to aspire.

Today's wedding industry, however, operates at a level of sophistication and with a degree of magnitude that makes the wedding industry of the 1950s seem quaint by comparison. Wedding-related marketing is everywhere, from "buff bride" workout routines ensuring upper-arm definition fit for a strapless gown to home equity lines of credit offered to a couple—or to their parents—as a means of affording an otherwise unaffordable reception. The volume of wedding-related products urged upon the newly engaged bride and groom—from the Yankee Candle Company's pillars scented with the company's proprietary Wedding Day fragrance to rice grains bred in the shape of hearts and crushable underfoot so as not to present a hazard to birds when thrown in the place of confetti—is breathtaking. And the pressure to mount a wedding that is not only a warm celebration among family and friends but also a spectacular and original event—one that promises to have family and friends talking about it for months afterward—is omnipresent, even for those whose budget or whose aspirations are modest, or who would like to think of themselves as eschewing wedding obsession.

It was my hope at the outset of reporting this book that by looking behind the scenes of the wedding industry and studying its grinding mechanics I might better understand why the American wedding is the way it is. But my interest in doing this was not, fundamentally, because I wanted to understand weddings themselves, which would be a limited if engaging goal. Nor was it because I wanted to malign the choices of individual brides and grooms. I enjoy a good wedding as much as the next person, and I have teared up even at ones I've attended—in the course of reporting this book—when the bride and groom have been strangers to me. I'm married, and I had a wedding of sorts, if not of the style or on the scale prescribed by the wedding industry. (I'll come back to that later.) Weddings are fun: a chance to dance to familiar tunes, to treat the senses with fresh flowers, to wear something other than jeans for a change. But the real reason weddings are compelling is that they are riven with human drama. I will not soon forget the breathtaking sight of one friend, a strong-willed, beautiful woman, alone on the dance floor with her father, a powerful businessman with whom she had a tempestuous relationship, the two of them swirling passionately (there is no other word for it) to the theme tune from *The Godfather.* Nor will I forget watching a crowd of stamping, cheering guests dancing the hora—the circle dance that is a staple at Jewish celebrations—for a quintessentially Waspy couple who had simply decided they liked the tradition and incorporated it into their wedding, which took place at the groom's family's home by a pond in a private residential enclave on Long Island, a setting that might have come from *The Great Gatsby*. The comedy and the pathos of family life are on display at a wedding, with short stories waiting to be written at every turn. I hope to be invited to many more of them.

My interest in the wedding industry, though, was driven by a conviction that weddings provide an unparalleled lens upon the intimate sphere of American life, and that the way we marry reveals a great deal about prevailing cultural expectations of love, hopes for marriage, and sense of the role of family. Weddings are often thought of as being only so much fluff and fun; but when looked at from the perspective of their larger cultural relevance they could hardly be more important, and more defining. It is a premise of this book that weddings are social events, as distinct from the private and always mysterious marriages that they inaugurate; and that they give expression, one way or another, to the values and preoccupations of the society in which they take place. Giving expression to social values is one of the things weddings are for, since good sense and an acquaintance with the relevant statistics might otherwise recommend that the compact of marriage be better undertaken in the sober contractual spirit currently reserved for the signing of divorce papers. We want weddings to be meaningful. But what, these days, do we make them mean?

An American wedding may be conducted in a church or temple, a hotel ballroom, a botanical garden, a restaurant, a private house, or, in one of those cases that seem contrived to elicit coverage in the local newspapers, in a hotair balloon or at the top of a ski slope. The couple getting married may be young, or middle-aged, or even elderly; they may have cohabited for years or may never have spent the night together. The wedding can last four hours on a Saturday afternoon, or it can fill a three-day weekend, with prewedding-day barbecue, postwedding-day brunch, and matching wedding-weekend T-shirts for all the guests. The ceremony can be performed by a priest or a rabbi or a judge; it can also, in some states, be performed by a notary public or simply by a friend of the bride and groom. It can cost a few hundred dollars in a Las Vegas chapel, or it can cost a few hundred thousand in the ballroom of the St. Regis hotel in New York, with floral installations by one of the city's top designers and a custom-designed cake as big as the Ritz, or even in the shape of the Ritz for that matter.

Although I speak in this book of the "American bride" or the "American wedding" there is, of course, no single, uniform American bride or American wedding about which generalizations can be made, or from which conclusions can be drawn. Or, it would be more accurate to say, the lack of uniformity among weddings in America is the contemporary American wedding's signal characteristic. While there are certain aspects of weddings that are almost universally observed among Americans (the bride's wearing of a white gown, the structure of a civil or religious ceremony followed by a reception with eating, drinking, and dancing) this basic template is applied in a dizzying variety of ways; and when I speak about the American wedding in general terms in this book, I do so with the knowledge that the range of American weddings is vast. There are about 2.3 million marriages in America every year, and no two weddings are exactly the same.

But while my observations may not apply to each of the weddings my reader has ever been to, it is my belief that they will ring true when applied to American weddings in the aggregate. The limitless nuptial possibility I have described above is, in a sense, the defining characteristic of the contemporary American wedding; just as limitless possibility—or the myth or promise of it, at least—is a defining characteristic of American life. The use of a wedding day as a vehicle for self-expression is an inevitable and distinctively

American tendency, and it is no surprise that Americans should take the opportunity to present themselves, on their wedding day, as more beautiful, better dressed, and wealthier than they are, or to try to incorporate something of their own tastes and personalities into the occasion, even if that amounts only to honoring the groom's preference for cupcakes over wedding cake, or the bride's wish to have her best male friend serve in the stead of a maid of honor.

But a wedding is also a profoundly conformist occasion, and one upon which the urge to observe some form of propriety is compellingly strong. It involves, after all, saying "I do" to the ruling principle of a society organized around legally contracted monogamous coupling, as well as to one's future spouse. Getting married is both one of the most conventional and one of the most exalted things a person can do; and while brides and grooms may pride themselves on their expressions of nuptial unconventionality, a wedding nonetheless prompts in its participants—the guests as well as the marrying couple—a desire to enact a role that has been scripted by some source more authoritative than their own powers of invention.

How to accommodate this desire in a culture in which novelty and innovation have become such irresistible forces does, however, present something of a challenge. To whom should Americans turn to be told how to get married? It is my contention that the wedding industry has eagerly stepped into this vacuum of authority, and that as a consequence the American wedding is shaped as much by commerce and marketing as it is by those influences couples might prefer to think of as affecting their nuptial choices, such as social propriety, religious observance, or familial expectation. Becoming engaged amounts to a change in one's social status—marking a departure from the ranks of the unattached—but it also marks the moment of transformation into a potential consumer of bridal products.

But there is much more at stake than the mere measurement of quantities of tulle produced for, and filet mignon consumed by, American brides, grooms, and their guests. While the wedding industry certainly moves a lot of product—it was estimated in 2006 that the wedding business was worth $161 billion to the United States economy—the most significant thing that the wedding industry is selling is fantasy, about the wedding day itself and the marriage that follows it. The foremost product peddled by the wedding industry is the notion that a wedding, if done right, will provide fulfillment of a hitherto unimagined degree, and will herald a similarly flawless marriage and a subsequent life of domestic contentment. From this perspective, naturally, doing a wedding right means doing it according to the wedding-industry playbook, with no expense spared and no bridal trifle uncoveted. If a bride buys into the wedding industry, she is promised the happily-ever-after that she, in her big white dress and tiara, deserves.

The perpetuation of this fantasy, it seems to me, is much more pernicious and damaging than any amount of havoc that might be wrought by a Bridezilla on a rampage. A bride who is gripped by the desire to have her guests' chair-backs tied with ribbons colored to coordinate precisely with the envelopes in which her save-the-date cards have been sent out can always laugh later at her own folly. But the bride who has been convinced, in some barely articulated but nonetheless persuasive sense, that coordinating her ribbons and her envelopes will contribute to the future harmony of her marriage has been sold not just an expensive complement of stationery but a dangerous bill of goods.

This book, then, comprises a journey through the wedding industry, exploring the degree to which weddings have been transformed by outside interests into machines for making money, as well as the ways in which those outside interests tap into the deepest hopes and fears of their consumers in order to accomplish their economic goals. I begin in chapter one with a look at the bridal media and at their influence in establishing what has come to be expected as standard at an American wedding, as well as their role in brokering relationships between brides and the businesses that serve them. In chapter two I look at the novel career calling of the professional wedding planner, and at the implications of handing over the conduct of weddings to hired hands. In chapter three I consider the importance of tradition when it comes to the practice of weddings, and the emotional uses to which the idea of tradition is pressed into service by all sorts of commercial interests, from the manufacturers of wedding favors to the Walt Disney Company and its Fairy Tale Weddings & Honeymoons program. Chapter four examines the iconic wedding product—the wedding gown—and traces it from the American aisle back to the Chinese factory floor.

Chapter five looks at the wedding registry, and the way in which department store conglomerates attempt to use the opportunity of a wedding to secure the bride as a customer for life. In chapter six I consider the role of religion in the contemporary wedding and look at the ways in which nuptial spirituality is marketed. In chapter seven I visit two wedding-industry towns, Gatlinburg, Tennessee, and Las Vegas, Nevada, to see how the business of weddings—in particular, the courtship of the so-called encore bride—is conducted when it constitutes an important part of a local economy. Chapter eight considers the wedding from the vantage point of retrospection, and examines how brides are offered the irresistible promise by wedding photographers and videographers that their wedding day, and its attendant emotions, need not be evanescent but can be permanently preserved and endlessly revisited. In chapter nine I turn to the honeymoon and consider the role the travel industry plays in establishing the idea that the contemporary wedding, and the marriage that follows it, is an individualistic adventure rather than a community sacrament. I conclude by turning to the bride herself and asking the surprisingly difficult question What, after all, is a wedding for?

This is a question that deserves consideration not just by individuals planning to wed, but by the rest of us as well, married or not. The American wedding—with its softball games, its matching linens, and its $161 billion industrial infrastructure—is an expression of this culture's character and a declaration from this culture's heart. The way we marry, for better or worse, is who we are; and if we were to reexamine our commitment to the American wedding as it currently exists, we might be surprised to find that our ultimate happiness does not depend upon it.

One

Weddings 101

"Who here has just got engaged?"

Dozens of slender arms shot up, and the diamonds on dozens of engagement rings suddenly sparkled in the bright morning light, like the flashbulbs of paparazzi cameras immortalizing a celebrity. I was seated in a wood-paneled library at the Whitney Museum of American Art on Madison Avenue in New York City, attending a seminar entitled "Inside Tips from the Editors of *Brides:* How to Avoid the Top Mistakes." It was well before the museum's usual opening time, and the luxury stores on the avenue were still shuttered from the night before; but in spite of the early hour, the room was filled to capacity with young women, none of whom seemed to have been too rushed to put on a lick of lip gloss and mascara before leaving her apartment or hotel room that morning. All were eagerly perched on chairs that had been set up in rows, their pens in hands and notebooks at the ready, as if attending a lecture at the optimistic outset of an academic term at a distinguished university.

The opening question, delivered by Millie Martini Bratten, the editor in chief of *Brides*, was a rhetorical one: Just about everyone present had just got engaged, the few exceptions being a handful of mothers-of-the-bride who held their pens and notebooks with an attentiveness equal to that of their daughters. The talk was part of the Wedding March on Madison, a weekend-long series of events cosponsored by the Madison Avenue Business Improvement District and Condé Nast, which publishes *Brides, Modern Bride,* and *Elegant Bride.* Brides-to-be had come from all over the country—thirty-three different states were represented—to take part, each paying $135 for the privilege.

Easily recognizable by the bright red tote bags filled with promotional literature and gifts they had been given upon registration, the Wedding Marchers could be seen over the course of the weekend trotting up and down Madison Avenue, sampling the wares. Bridal fashions were on show at The Pierre hotel; Steuben Glass hosted a cocktail party; Ghurka luggage was raffling off a honeymoon in Los Cabos, Mexico. La Maison du Chocolat had a tasting; Williams-Sonoma held a cooking demonstration; and Frette, the purveyor of high-end linens, offered one-on-one consultations advising potential customers how to go about "building a trousseau," as the Wedding March calendar put it.

In addition to the shopping opportunities, there was a raft of panel discussions and presentations on subjects ranging from wedding etiquette to choosing a wedding cake to executing the perfect updo, all presented by experts from the top of the field, such as Preston Bailey, an event designer and wedding-guide author, who showed images of his work that included an arrangement of roses in the shape of a five-foot-tall pineapple and another large floral arrangement in the shape of a cow. (That event, at the Carlyle hotel's appropriately named Trianon Suite, was full to capacity.) It was as if the pages of *Brides* magazine had been brought to life up and down the avenue: Everything was glossy and perfectly presented, from the gowns at the Vera Wang boutique to the diamond baubles at Cartier to the well-groomed salespeople behind each cash register.

The Wedding March provided an immersion course in the preoccupations of the modern bride, or at least in the preoccupations of the ideal reader of the bridal magazines sponsoring the event; and demonstrated how the bridal media were reaching out to their readership beyond the pages of a magazine. The academic analogy had apparently occurred to Peter K. Hunsinger, then the president of the Condé Nast Bridal Group, who had announced that the Wedding March would provide an attendee with an opportunity to "get her MBA in getting married"; although it seemed likely to me that the single slim volume a bride would be turning to most often during the course of her education would be her checkbook.

The audience members at the Inside Tips seminar at the Whitney were certainly eager to learn from the editors of *Brides*, and were full of questions. How far in advance should a bride start getting facials? As soon as she is engaged, said Denise O'Donoghue, the magazine's beauty and jewelry director. "Just know that planning a wedding is going to be stressful, so take your fiancé for a massage," Donoghue advised. "You have to involve them in things that are fun for them. The thing to do is to enjoy your engagement period, so you have that glow." Should a bride register for an engagement party as well as for the wedding? She should register for everything, said Donna Ferrari, the magazine's tabletop, food, and wine director. "Registering for gifts is one of the most indispensable tools in the entire wedding process," said Ferrari. "It is a convenience and a courtesy to your guests. You can set up an account with a bank for a mortgage; you can register for sports equipment, for luggage, for tablewares. It lets you perpetuate old traditions, and create new ones. Start the registry process months ahead. Twirl those forks; bring swatches; have a clip book. A lot of people are going to say, 'We don't need all that stuff.' You do."

Becoming a bride, it was clear, was a project that demanded much more of a woman than merely saying "I do" to her intended. The way that the editors of *Brides* made it appear, planning a wedding would demand hours of time and advanced organizational skills. What should a bride wear if her ceremony is in the morning but her reception isn't until the evening, one audience member asked Rachel Leonard, the magazine's fashion director. She'll probably need two different wedding gowns, Leonard responded: a formal one for the ceremony and a sexier one for night. At this suggestion, some in even the seminar's compliant audience balked, and one listener suggested that an alternative solution might be to make do with a single gown with a bolero jacket or detachable train. The look on Leonard's face was such as might be made by the sommelier at Le Bernadin when faced with a request for a bottle of Yellow Tail chardonnay.

Leonard had a long list of tips for avoiding wedding-dress disaster—necessary counsel for women who never before, and never again, would wear a gown so demanding. "I would recommend choosing your site before you choose your dress," she advised, as the brides scribbled notes. "It would be inappropriate having a beach dress going down the aisle of a cathedral. It's a mistake to order a dress in a small size, assuming that you're going to lose weight. Remember to step into your dress *after* you've put on your makeup. And you'd better practice dancing in your dress, and practice walking in it. Always walk forward, not backward: If you have a train and walk backward, you'll kill yourself." The image of back-stepping brides keeling fatally over was, to be sure, a sobering one to contemplate.

In spite of the suggestion that the Wedding March would provide participants with their "MBA in getting married," the educational experience it most resembled was a crash course at a finishing school offering lessons in manners and comportment. To promote it as such would, of course, have been much less persuasive to its target demographic: The concept of finishing school would appear old-fashioned and even mildly degrading to today's confident young women. But becoming a bride—at least becoming the kind of bride featured in bridal magazines—does require the acquisition of skills and savoir faire that formerly were the expected endowment of privileged girlhood but in which the modern woman is quite unaccomplished and for which she is quite unprepared. When else has a contemporary woman had to consider whether a basque or an Empire waist will be more becoming to her figure, or to know the difference between a sweetheart and a Sabrina neckline? When has she been obliged to compose an invitation or to stand in a receiving line? When before has a woman for whom lunch probably consists of a sandwich been required to select sterling-silver flatware offered in five-piece place settings? Every contemporary woman's transformation into bride is a Pygmalion story.

For help in such matters, she turns to the bridal magazines, which typically serve as a young woman's first point of entry into the world of weddings once it has been determined she is to participate in one. The experience of buying one's first bridal magazine—like the experience of stepping into a formal gown for the first time—can be disorienting in the extreme. Its pages offer both the seductive pleasure of taking up what may be a long-anticipated role and the shock of realizing just what enacting that role is going to require in terms of money, time, and energy expended. Young women today often refer to bridal magazines as "wedding porn," and the analogy—with its suggestion that the contents of bridal magazines are somewhat illicit, eminently compulsive, and pathologically fantastical—is a good one. Bridal magazines offer an invitation into a fantasy world, but the editorial tone they strike is one of the utmost practicality, as if there were nothing the least bit extraordinary about decorating the entryway of a church with topiary obelisks and a carpet of moss, or selecting as one's own "signature hors d'oeuvre" a bite-sized pizza topped with cranberry, smoked mozzarella, and thyme and served in a miniature monogrammed pizza box.

A newly engaged woman—or one who suspects that she is about to become newly engaged and wants to get a jump on her preparations—is faced with an array of glossy magazines to serve as reference guides: *Brides, Modern Bride, Elegant Bride, Bridal Guide, InStyle Weddings, Martha Stewart Weddings, The Knot Weddings*, as well as numerous local titles—*New Jersey Bride, Cape Cod Bride*—and the bridal editions of magazines with which she may already be familiar, such as *New York* or *Town & Country*. That is a lot of magazines to choose from, but the real challenge, like choosing between one brand of spaghetti sauce and another, is to distinguish the differences among them. The similarity of content is overwhelming: Rare is the bridal magazine that does not reference, either by name or by image, Audrey Hepburn or Grace Kelly, and if there were to be a moratorium placed on the use of the phrase "simple elegance," they would all be forced out of business.

It is, though, possible to determine some distinctions, if you look closely enough. *Modern Bride* is aimed at the young woman with more fashion-forward tastes—the kind of person who might think of brightening up her centerpieces by sticking zebra tomatoes and fresh peas in among the flowers. *Brides* offers a more classic nuptial style and, with cover lines such as "Marrying at 20, 30, 40!" and "The Best Dresses for Brides of All Ages," takes care to address not just the typical first-time bride but also speaks to a reader long past the first blush of youth. Among the more novel additions to the bridal shelf is *Martha Stewart Weddings*, which brings Stewart's do-it-yourself fanaticism to nuptial preparation, offering suggestions such as the substitution of lavender stalks for cocktail stirrers. Another relative newcomer to the field, *InStyle Weddings*, which was launched in 2000, offers friendly, consensual coverage of celebrity weddings in combination with product placement, so a reader may choose orchids for her centerpieces on the strength of knowing that Demi Moore and Ashton Kutcher also did so, or may have her and her husband's initials spelled out in Swarovski crystals on the soles of her bridal shoes, like the singer Pink did.

The bridal media are not limited to magazines: Wedding-planning Web sites have become a significant competitor for the attention of brides since their establishment in the late nineties. The Web site of The Knot offers, in addition to the kind of editorial content typically found in magazines, online tools such as budget calculators, serves as a portal for wedding-related online shopping, and has built an enormous community of brides who contribute to its message boards. (The categories on these include "Reception Ideas," "Wedding Woes," and "Mothers of the Bride and Groom"; questions asked range from where to buy a rubber stamp decorated with a custom monogram to whether it's appropriate for a groom to invite an ex-girlfriend to the wedding.) By 2006 the site was getting more than 2 million unique visitors per month, while the circulation of *Brides* at the end of 2005 was just 370,000, which explains why, in 2006, Condé Nast launched Brides.com, a Web site combining content from all its bridal magazines as well as new content created for the Web, in its own pursuit of the online reader.

Print magazines and interactive Web sites offer the bride quite different experiences: For one thing, it's easier for a woman with an office job surreptitiously to take time out from the workday to plan her wedding online than it is for her to hide a five-hundred-page magazine on her lap under her desk. (So much easier, in fact, that a few years ago the Calvin Klein company, which employs many young women of marriageable age, established a firewall on its computer network to prevent its employees' accessing The Knot. Wedding porn indeed.) But while the means of delivery may be radically different, the bridal fantasy promoted online and on the page is very similar. It is also more complex than immediately meets the eye.

The immediate promise is that of being the girl in the big white dress at the center of everyone's attention. The bride in white appears on the cover of every issue of every bridal magazine with an invariance that must tax even the most ingenious of art directors; and some art directors seem to have given up even a faint pretense of ingenuity. (The covers of the June/July 2005 and the June/July 2006 issues of *Modern Bride* are almost identical, featuring exactly the same model with her hair in almost exactly the same upswept style, wearing in both pictures a strapless gown and a veil, and posed in both cases in front of a dazzling blue ocean and enticing blue sky. The only real difference is that the 2005 dress cost about $3,000 while the 2006 one, a mass-market brand, cost only about $850.) While other magazines are constantly chasing after the new to hold on to the readers whose attention they've already captured, the editors of bridal magazines know that last year's reader will not be this year's reader, and so content can be recycled endlessly. There will always be a reader for whom the six-month countdown calendar is exciting, fresh, and new.

But the promise of being center stage for a day is not all a bridal magazine has to offer—that, after all, tends to be the prerogative of any bride, no matter how much effort she puts into her gown or hair-styling choices. What the bridal magazines promote in addition is the idea that a bride deserves to be the center of attention for the entire period of her engagement—which, according to industry estimates, lasts about sixteen or seventeen months. She deserves to be the center of her own attention, at least. For the sixteen months of her engagement it is her privilege, her right—indeed, her obligation—to become preoccupied with herself, her appearance, her tastes, and her ability to showcase them to their best advantage. Being a bride, according to the bridal media's prescription, amounts to a quest for self-perfection, or perfection of the outward self at least. "Girls use their engagement as a kind of transition—a stage of life, a time for self-improvement," Nina Lawrence, then the publisher of *Brides* magazine, told me a few days after the Wedding March on Madison. Getting married provides an opportunity to revisit every failed New Year's resolution and, this time, to succeed.

The notion that a wedding amounts to a transition between one stage of life and another is a well-established anthropological observation, and one for which Arnold van Gennep coined the term *rite of passage* in 1908. A rite of passage, as van Gennep characterized it, is a means for a society to mark an individual's movement from one stage of life to another, or from one social status to another; such rites permit the society to manage changes in the status of its constituents without the structure of the society itself coming under threat.

The idea of the wedding as a necessary rite of passage has gained common currency in our own society, but the passage marked by the contemporary wedding is very different from that of the societies upon which van Gennep based his theory. The wedding does not signify a transition to adulthood: In 2004 the median age among first-time American brides was almost twenty-six, and among first-time grooms it was just shy of twenty-seven and a half—ages at which even those most committed to immaturity find it hard to sustain the exclusive pursuits of adolescence. It does not herald the start of an active sexual life: A study released in 2004 by the Department of Health showed that by the age of nineteen, 69 percent of girls and 64 percent of boys had experienced sexual intercourse. It does not mark the departure from the childhood home of either bride or groom: According to a 2002 report from the Centers for Disease Control, 38 percent of women aged between twenty and twenty-four have cohabited at some point in their lives, while multitudes more have lived with roommates or alone for years before marrying.

What passage, then, does a contemporary woman's engagement amount to? What transition does she undergo? From the perspective of the bridal media and the wedding industry they represent, there's a simple answer to that question: She becomes a new kind of consumer. The Wedding March, Nina Lawrence reported with satisfaction when we had lunch, had been a huge success: Seven hundred brides had participated in more than eighty events, and the retailers who had taken part had, she said, been overwhelmed by the response. "We have done something to get consumers to their stores—to tie the retailers to the wedding experience," Lawrence said. "The girls this weekend—they just walked to the cash registers. The stores didn't know what to do with them all. You usually only see business like this in the two weeks before Christmas."

The transition undergone by the contemporary young woman who is marrying for the first time is, in fundamental ways, much less significant than that experienced by her forebears: Her life as a wife may not be very different from her life preengagement, in practical terms. But the passage that is passed in the imagination can be profound, and it is upon the bride's expectation of the impending transformation of her inward self, to be accomplished through the outward accumulation of stuff, that the bridal media work. The bridal march toward the cash registers on Madison Avenue is not driven by a mindless consumerism on the part of the young women in attendance but by the fervent hope that by entering into the program of self-improvement prescribed by the editors of *Brides* in the Whitney seminar—by getting monthly facials, and registering for fine china, and practicing the avoidance of reverse perambulation in a bridal gown—a new self will emerge. This self will be one whose skin always glows with happiness, whose life is one of such grace that the fine china will always be in use, and whose progress will never be backward but always forward and upward, to ever greater heights of joy and satisfaction.

The bridal magazines have been so constitutive of the wedding industry, and have served so unwaveringly to further its interests, that it is fair to say there would be no wedding industry without them. The oldest bridal magazine in the country is *Brides*, which was founded in 1934 under the title *So You're Going to Be Married* and was initially sent free of charge to those women in New York, New Jersey, and Connecticut whose engagements were announced in the newspapers' society pages. (It later became *The Bride's Magazine*, then *Bride's*; the apostrophe was dropped in 2005.) "We sincerely hope this magazine will be inviting and charming and gladden hearts already gladdened by that lovely thing called Love," the magazine's first editor said of her publication.

The hearts of readers were not, however, the only constituency for which the magazine was intended. Its creator, one Wells Drorbaugh, was the advertising manager for *House & Garden* and was inspired to create his new magazine by an article in *Fortune*, which noted that even at times of economic depression people could be relied upon to spend money on weddings. Courting advertisers, and serving as a delivery system of brides to advertisers, is still the mission of *Brides* and its fellow magazines, as well as of the rival online publications. "At the end of the day, what we're delivering is access to this audience" is how David Liu, C.E.O. of The Knot, put it to me. (Liu's delivery of that access, he explained, could be conducted with a much greater degree of specificity than that offered by the traditional bridal magazines, since readers registering on his site provide their wedding date and other useful information: "We will target our travel advertising and messaging to hit in the six- to five-month mark prior to the person's wedding, saying, 'Hey, you know what? You're about six months out, and believe it or not, it's time to plan your honeymoon—and by the way, here are some offers from select sponsors.")

One of the ways in which the fidelity of the bridal media to the interests of their advertisers is demonstrated is in the annual production by the Condé Nast Bridal Group of its American Wedding Study. (The Condé Nast Bridal Group is the umbrella title for *Brides, Modern Bride, Elegant Bride,* and Brides.com.) This is a summary of the state of the American wedding based upon a survey of brides-to-be, and its central finding, the average cost of an American wedding, is reported each year in the news media. (The results of the study are released in time for what is thought of as the "wedding season" of May and June, even though there is in fact no sharp spike in the number of weddings at that time of year, more of a gentle rise.) Every year, as might be expected, the American Wedding Study's tally of the amount spent by Americans on getting married increases: from about $22,000 in 2003 to more than $26,000 in 2005 to, in 2006, a grand total of $27,852.

The details of the American Wedding Study suggest that today's bride is embracing her role in exactly the spirit of consumer ebullience that was being promoted at the Wedding March on Madison and that is encouraged in the pages of the bridal magazines. According to the 2006 study, Americans were spending $14 billion annually on engagement rings, wedding rings, and other items of jewelry. They were purchasing just over $7 billion worth of wedding gowns, tuxedos, flower girl outfits, bridesmaids' dresses, veils, satin shoes, gloves, stoles, and other items of wedding attire. Brides and grooms were registering for $9 billion worth of gifts from their friends and relatives, of whom there were an average of 165 at each wedding. The expenses of the wedding day itself, including the food and drink, the limousines, the flowers, the wedding bands, and other nuptial paraphernalia, totaled $39 billion, which comes to $750,000 being spent on weddings across America every weekend (with the exception of Super Bowl weekend, when only the oblivious or highly inconsiderate decide to begin married life). A further $8.5 billion were being spent on honeymoon vacations. And, in the glow of the first few months of marriage, American newlyweds could be expected to spend more than $42 billion on buying or leasing a new car, nearly $20 billion on insurance, $15 billion on financial services, $4.5 billion on furniture, and almost $4 billion on tableware, silverware, and other items for their new family home.

One of the interesting things about the American Wedding Study is that it reports the vast and rising costs of getting married not with disapproval but with enthusiasm. This, when you think about it, is a curious stance to be taken by a group of consumer magazines—at least it might seem that way from the perspective of a reader of *Brides* or *Modern Bride,* for whom the news that the average cost of a wedding has increased nearly 100 percent since 1990, a fact trumpeted in the 2006 press release, is hardly a cause for celebration. What is doubly interesting, from this point of view, is that the figures used in the American Wedding Study have not been adjusted for inflation, and so the difference between 1990 expenses and 2006 expenses seems all the greater due to the rise in the cost of living. If you run the numbers through the U.S. Department of Labor's Consumer Price Index inflation calculator, the cost of a wedding in 1990—$15,280—would have a purchasing power in 2006 of $23,562. Looked at this way, the cost of a wedding has only increased 18 percent between 1990 and 2006, which is much more cheering news for today's newly engaged men and women, but not, of course, for the advertisers on behalf of whom the Wedding Study is produced.

The American Wedding Study has become indispensable to anyone writing about the wedding business—or considering making an investment in it—because it has inserted itself into an informational vacuum. The government does not collect any data about wedding costs or practices, beyond the raw numbers of marriages that take place each year (2,230,000 in 2005, the most recent year for which figures are available). And so while one can turn to the Department of Labor's Bureau of Labor Statistics for data on the amount the average American spends per year upon education ($950 in 2004), dairy products ($371), and public transportation ($441), for data about weddings there is really no source other than the wedding industry itself.

This, inevitably, has an influence on the way in which the data are gathered and disseminated. The 1,619 respondents to the survey upon which the American Wedding Study of 2006 was based were reached because they had, at some point, made themselves known to the Bridal Group by answering a survey online, or responding to a magazine promotion, or attending a bridal show. They had, in other words, already demonstrated an interest in having the kind of wedding that bridal magazines promote. (A bride whose wedding plans consist of making a trip to City Hall would most likely not have been reached by the survey.)

There is, of course, no way of knowing whether the results of a survey conducted with more scrupulous objectivity would be very different, and such a survey would be extremely difficult to conduct, since there exists no National Registry of the Affianced to which a polling organization can turn for a list of brides-to-be. For the purposes of the wedding industry, it does not much matter that the respondents have already indicated their interest in acquiring the products and services the wedding industry is providing, since the brides the industry is interested in reaching are those who *do* want the dress, the flowers, the jewelry, the honeymoon, and all the other conventional trappings of bridehood. But this means that the "average" wedding of which the industry speaks is average only to the extent that it represents the wedding practices of readers of bridal magazines.

I've already cited the Condé Nast Bridal Group's figure for the total expenditure on weddings in America—$161 billion—and I will be referring to their figures again. The Condé Nast figures are, unfortunately, the best that are available, and whatever their limitations in indicating the choices of all American brides, they are extremely useful for indicating the directions in which the wedding industry seeks to turn the attention of brides. But when in this book I have used the wedding industry's statistics I have done so in a spirit of skepticism and with full consciousness of their provenance, and I caution my reader to approach them similarly. For example that $161 billion figure includes not just the costs of the wedding day but also the cost of the honeymoon, the cost of gifts bought for the couple through their bridal registry, and the amount spent by newlyweds on furniture, cars, insurance, and financial services. (If you discount the nonnuptial, postwedding expenses, the amount spent nationally on weddings, including registry and honeymoons, comes to $83 billion: still a huge amount, but at least slightly more modest.)

The larger figure depends on quite a stretch of the definition of wedding-related expenditures—at least it looks that way, unless you are an advertising executive at an automobile company or a bank looking for ways to reach potential new consumers for your products, in which case it seems no stretch at all.

What does all this wedding-industry hype mean for the woman who turns to the bridal magazines for guidance and inspiration? One of the things it means is that an expectation that getting married is going to be a very costly endeavor has been drummed into her head well in advance of the start of her wedding planning. (In fact, her expenses may well be higher than the averages given in the American Wedding Study: In New York City the figure may easily be twice the reported national average.) If a bride has been told, repeatedly, that it costs nearly $28,000 to have a wedding, then she starts to think that spending nearly $28,000 on a wedding is just one of those things a person has to do, like writing a rent check every month or paying health insurance premiums. (Or she prides herself on being a budget bride and spending a mere $15,000 on the event.) She is less likely to reflect upon the fact that $28,000 would cover an awful lot of rent checks or health insurance payments; that, in fact, $28,000 would have more than covered a 10 percent down payment on the median purchase price of a house in 2005 and would cover the average cost to a family of a health insurance policy, at 2005 rates, for a decade. The bride who has been persuaded that $28,000 is a reasonable amount of money to spend on her wedding day is less likely to measure that total against the nation's median household income—$42,389 in 2004—and reflect upon whether it is, in fact, reasonable for her or for anyone to spend the equivalent of seven and a half months of the average American's salary on one day's celebration.

But establishing the bride's expectation of astronomical wedding expenses is only one effect of the wedding industry's broadcasting of escalating wedding costs. Another effect is that, by exaggerating the scale and scope of the wedding industry—or, at least, putting the rosiest possible gloss on the available statistics—the wedding industry actually increases its scale and scope. By promoting the notion that American brides have billions of dollars at their disposal, the wedding industry invites yet more businesses to join the party.

This means that the American bride is beset by proliferating suggestions of ways to spend her $28,000 or more. The range of products and services available to her is seemingly limitless in quantity and ingenuity. Dance studios, such as the Fred Astaire Dance Studios in New York City, offer "first dance" classes that include not only instruction in the appropriate steps and gestures, but also the opportunity for brides and grooms to attend practice parties at which professional dancers help alleviate their social anxiety. An association of wedding service providers called the Boston Wedding Group hosts something called a Bridal Survival Club, which offers support-group meetings for overwhelmed brides-to-be to meet and commiserate—and, not coincidentally, to sample the wares offered by members of the Boston Wedding Group. At the Amansala resort in Tulum, Mexico, brides-to-be can attend a prewedding yoga retreat, with calming meditation and muscle-tone-improving exercise. The American Laser Center offers prewedding permanent hair removal. And on and on, ad nuptial infinitum.

What part, then, do bridal magazines play in encouraging the development of this Bridezilla culture, in which wedding obsession is mandated of all newly engaged women? The message that the bridal magazines convey to their readers is that a wedding is a consumer rite of passage, in which the taking up of a new role in life is given material substance through the acquisition of products and services for both the wedding itself and for the marriage that is to follow. But no one is actually forcing brides to become the wedding-crazed consumers that are the bridal magazines' ideal readership, and the eagerness with which couples embrace the protocols established by the bridal media cannot simply be explained by their market availability. To be sure, wedding consumers, like all consumers, are very vulnerable to persuasion; but that persuasion, to be most effective, must speak to some sense of need.

It came to seem to me, as I attended the Wedding March on Madison and read the bridal magazines and studied the statistical reports that their publishers produce in pursuit of advertisers, that the stress of planning a wedding by the book—of acquiring all the right accessories and of staging an event that approximates those portrayed in airbrushed perfection in the bridal media—functions as a substitute for the experience of trauma that once was an essential and unavoidable part of the wedding rite of passage. No longer do newlyweds have to negotiate the shock of the transition from the parental home to the marital one; nor face the virginal intimidations of the marriage bed; nor cope with the responsibilities of housekeeping or breadwinning for the first time.

But while the distinction between unmarried and married life has become so much less momentous, the wedding itself has become far more so. Brides and grooms expect that their wedding will demand months of stressful, time-consuming planning. There will almost invariably be conflict between husband- and wife-to-be, as well as between themselves and their families. The process will be financially burdensome beyond many couples' means. It is as if the bygone traumas that were a necessary part of the life of a newlywed have been transferred and transformed into the new, invented traumas of planning a wedding. Surviving the wedding and its preparations has become the first test of a couple's compatibility while under duress: "I just keep telling myself if we can get through this, we can get through anything," wrote one participant on a wedding-planning Internet discussion board. (She was contributing to a thread entitled "Anyone else wish it were over with?")

With the transition into marriage meaning so much less than it once did, the preparation for a wedding must be made to mean so much more. Being a bride is no longer merely a transitional state, in the way that van Gennep would have understood it, and as the term was once applied: a brief incarnation between the more definitive and meaningful categories of being unmarried and being married. Being a bride has become a category in and of itself, an *occupation*—one that requires tutelage at the hands of experts whose curriculum has been established with the interests of an ever-expanding wedding industry foremost in mind.

The textbooks of that curriculum are the bridal magazines, with special educational sessions like the Wedding March on Madison available for extra credit. And the brides at the Wedding March who returned to the Whitney museum for a cocktail reception with a keynote address by Vera Wang after a long day of browsing and shopping up and down the avenue had absorbed its lessons. "My friend spent four hundred dollars on Bobbi Brown products yesterday, and then when she went for a makeup consultation this morning they told her all different colors," one young woman said to another, as she changed out of flat Chinese slippers and into high heels on the sidewalk. Another said to a friend, "I always said, when I get married, I want a plain white dress, and now it's all changed—I want off-white; I want lace; I want rhinestones."

After attending the Wedding March on Madison and hearing conversations like these, I thought it was time to look behind the scenes of the wedding industry—to go to the places and talk to the people with whom the bride herself has little contact but whose business imperatives have such an impact upon the way in which she will wed. As I did so, I had in mind another comment I had come across by Peter K. Hunsinger, the Condé Nast executive who had compared the Wedding March to an MBA program. This time, Hunsinger had offered an image that was considerably less flattering. The bride, he told a newspaper interviewer, is "kind of the ultimate consumer, the drunken sailor. Everyone is trying to get to her."

Was that so, I wondered? And if it was, who was pouring the drinks?

Two

The Business of Brides

A few years ago the Association of Bridal Consultants held a conference in San Antonio, Texas, and a social event took place one evening at a southwestern-style restaurant during which the guests were, in festive Mexican style, invited to take a whack at a piñata. The piñata had been strung up from the ceiling and decorated to represent a "bride from hell," complete with a pitchfork, horns, and a tail, and as each of the association members stepped up to take her turn, fueled by tequila and long-buried resentment, she yelled out the name of her most annoyingly picky or irredeemably cheap or frustratingly indecisive client. Whenever Gerard J. Monaghan, the cofounder of the Association of Bridal Consultants, tells this story—it is one of his favorites—he shakes his head and chuckles indulgently. "I have never seen so much anger and aggression expressed by a group of women," he says.

I first heard about the piñata from Monaghan during the twentieth annual Business of Brides conference of the association, which was being held in Kansas City, Missouri, over a bleak weekend in November. I went to the conference because the association is one of the leading professional bodies for workers in the wedding industry, and it would, I thought, be a good place to start discovering how the American bride appears to those who cater to her. At the conference, which was abuzz with wedding planners and would-be wedding planners attending networking lunches and educational seminars, I hoped to begin to understand the American wedding industry from the inside out.

Which is how I found myself, one dismal, rainy evening, at a wedding venue on the outskirts of Kansas City called Meadowview Gardens, attending a sixties-themed barbecue with a large crowd of ebullient off-duty wedding planners. The Garden Room, where the party took place, might have served equally well under different circumstances as a greenhouse, with wide expanses of storm-slashed windows, a vaulted roof with aluminum beams around which lengths of white tulle had been wrapped, and gleaming white floor tiles. A long table at the center of the room was set with steaming chafing dishes full of smoky, sauce-smothered barbecued pork slices and pieces of chicken, and an indoor fountain tinkled in a corner like a forgotten faucet. Most of the available floor space was jammed with large, circular tables, though there was an area set aside for dancing to a selection of wedding-reception favorites, such as "The Twist." The proprietress, Nancy Jarvis-Vogel, who was wearing a vivid pink mother-of-the-bride suit reminiscent of Jackie Kennedy's outfit on the Zapruder film, explained that construction on Meadowview Gardens had only just been completed and urged her guests to step outside to inspect her ceremonial gazebo. "I've got eighty-five thousand dollars' worth of concrete out there," she said, which hardly seemed sufficient incentive to make the excursion.

Most of the wedding planners in attendance had embraced the costume-party directive with gusto. One wan young woman, whose pale hair hung in contrived lankness around her face and who introduced herself to everybody as Moonchild, wore a sackcloth gown embroidered with flowers, apparently a relic from a wedding circa 1972. Another was dressed like an extra from the movie *Hairspray,* in a miniskirt, black go-go boots, and a blond bobbed wig. A member of a delegation of wedding planners from Japan was dressed as Astro Girl, the Japanese anime character, in a red polka-dot dress and red boots. The association's then director of corporate relations, David M. Wood III, was making his way around the room in a very jolly fashion, dressed in a black leather jacket and wearing a rubbery Elvis mask.

Jerry Monaghan is tall and hearty, and his costume consisted of a plaid shirt that referenced the wholesome *Leave It to Beaver* start of the decade rather than its degenerate conclusion. After I had grabbed a glass of fruity red wine from the bar, I found him standing under an arbor decked with flowers in the corner of the room, surveying the scene with satisfaction. He and his wife, Eileen, had run the Association of Bridal Consultants since 1981, and business was booming. "We now have 3,686 members, and that's up 25 percent in the last eleven months," he said. "Do you realize how many people are successful consultants because we have provided them with education and support?"

Weddings, Monaghan told me as we stood by the arbor, were no longer family events, planned by the bride and her mother. They were big productions, requiring the services of experienced professionals. And the profile of those professionals was changing, too. "It's not the little ladies, the church social secretaries with the phone book anymore," he told me. "There are more men, and more straight men. There are more business degrees. The industry is changing, and people are realizing that this is a legitimate business." It was his ultimate hope, he explained, to bring together all the wedding-related trade associations into one large organization that would represent wedding-industry interests and create prowedding advertising campaigns. "It will be like the 'Got Milk?' commercials," he explained. "'Got a Wedding Professional?'"

Why, I asked Monaghan, was there a need for wedding professionals in the first place? At that, he called over Eileen, a tall woman with vivid red-tinted hair who had been standing a few steps away, chatting with Elvis. "Give her your list of reasons," he said. Eileen, who had the title of vice president of the association, launched into what sounded like a well-rehearsed spiel, referencing figures from what was at the time the most recent Condé Nast survey.

"First, it's a $120-billion-dollar industry, with the wedding day totaling 50 billion of that," she said. "You have an older bride and groom, and they are more sophisticated. Then, it's a more mobile society—people don't get married where they grew up anymore. And there isn't a nuclear family anymore, so people don't have Uncle Joe take the pictures, or Aunt Sally bake the cake. Another thing you've got to remember about weddings now is that a lot of the people getting married are the children of divorce. They saw what happened to their parents and they think, 'If I have a bigger ceremony, I will have a bigger commitment.' Plus, this is their only big party, and they want to do it right. They are older, and they want more stuff."

"They want two hundred of their friends, and food they can't even pronounce," Jerry added, with a wry smile at the follies of youth.

By now, Elvis had made his way over to join us. "It seems like the less money people have, the more they spend," he said, cheerfully.

I would have liked to ask the Monaghans more questions—and to have heard more about their own wedding, which, Jerry started telling me, took place in 1981 on a very low budget, with not a wedding professional in sight—but our conversation was halted when we had to surrender the arbor to the association's Colorado chapter, the members of which had, in the spirit of adolescent summer campers, prepared a comedy skit for the entertainment of their colleagues. Naturally, the skit involved the reenactment of a wedding. The bride, a wedding planner who was more than old enough to be a mother of the bride, was wearing an enormous, shiny white gown that had a soufflé of petticoats and was constructed on a scale approaching that of the bridal gown worn by Princess Diana. Her groom—actually a wedding photographer—wore a neat white suit. The pair took their places under the arbor, in front of the minister, another association colleague in borrowed robes, who asked whether anyone present knew of any impediment to the marriage.

At this, the *Hairspray* extra leaped to her go-go-booted feet with a squeal. "I do! He was engaged to me!" she said. "And he slept with me last night!" The bride turned on the groom with a red-faced fury that seemed more petulant than brokenhearted, like a middle-aged Veruca Salt in white satin. "I can't believe you did this to me!" she cried as she hurled her bouquet into the crowd of delighted onlookers. "I was going to marry you even if you didn't have money!"

There was much applause as the skit ended—more for effort, it seemed, than for conception or execution—and then the DJ cued up "Hound Dog." Elvis jived forward and took the bride's hand, and she hiked her train up around her waist and hopped around in her exposed crinoline. The next song was "The Loco-Motion," and as all the wedding planners formed a conga line and wound their way around the room, hooting and cheering, I found myself thinking of Arnold van Gennep, the anthropologist, and picturing the planners as a tribal hunting party, vigorously enacting the imagined slaughter of a deer and engaging in a ritual dance before going forth to rain arrows down upon whatever unlucky wildlife happened across their path.

As Jerry Monaghan's piñata anecdote and the Colorado chapter's skit suggested, the bride is a less enchanting figure to those who depend upon her for their livelihoods—and for whom Bridezilla culture is a daily reality—than she is to those on her wedding-day guest list. Bridezilla culture, though, is exactly what members of the Association of Bridal Consultants thrive upon, since the more complex and elaborate the wedding plans, the greater the need for professional help in executing them. As far as members of the Association of Bridal Consultants are concerned, the bride from hell is at least preferable to the bride from City Hall.

The Association of Bridal Consultants is a national organization for professional wedding planners that claims a membership of nearly four thousand. Wedding planners (or wedding consultants, or wedding coordinators, as they are sometimes known) help brides and grooms navigate the business of preparing for a wedding, serving much as a general contractor does on a house renovation project. (They can also provide what is known as "day-of" service, which means that while they have had no hand in the planning of the wedding, they are there on the day to make sure that the event proceeds according to a prescribed timeline.) The number of professional wedding planners is increasing—Jerry Monaghan estimates there are now about ten thousand of them nationally—and their use by brides has become more widespread, thanks in part to their endorsement in the pages of bridal magazines: The 2006 American Wedding Study from Condé Nast reported that 18 percent of its respondents had engaged the services of a professional wedding planner.

A detailed profile of the professional wedding planner's potential client was provided in Kansas City by Antonia van der Meer, the editor in chief of *Modern Bride* magazine and the conference's keynote speaker. Soigné in knee-high boots, a kicky skirt, and a turtleneck, as if she were the slightly older, married sister of a character on *Sex and the City*, van der Meer spoke in the Fairmont hotel's ballroom on the first morning of the conference. Her subject was the Echo Boom—the children of Baby Boomers, born between 1979 and 2002—and the opportunity they were about to present to the wedding industry, if the wedding industry was prepared to market to them intelligently.

The oldest members of this generation were now twenty-five years old—or, as van der Meer put it, "The leading edge of the Echo Boom is now moving into the engagement zone." The potential pool of engaged consumers was projected to grow 30 percent in the next fifteen years to a high of over 4.2 million. "That's good news for all of us," she said, as she cataloged the psychographics of this enticing new consumer. Events and social shifts that struck the older among her audience as radical changes were all that the Echo Boom generation had ever known: "Grace Kelly, Elvis Presley, Karen Carpenter—they've always been dead," van der Meer said. These young brides didn't remember Red China, or renting phones from AT&T instead of buying them, or Coors beer being unavailable east of the Mississippi River, or a time when there were two superpowers.

Members of the Echo Boom, van der Meer explained, do not share the antiestablishment tendencies of their parents, or of Generation X, the demographic cohort born in the years after the Baby Boom ended. "Their top three life goals are to get a well-paying job, have a good relationship with their parents, and get married," she said. "They are the best-educated and best-behaved generation, and they like to follow the rules." They are also the most sheltered generation ever, having been driven around in cars bearing BABY ON BOARD signs while wearing five-point safety harnesses; and they have been pressured to excel by their Boomer parents, doing two hours of homework a night while still in elementary school. Even love is different for members of the Echo Boom. Sex, through which their parents' generation sought liberation, has a darker connotation now: For them, a world without the threat of AIDS is as unimaginable as a world without the nationwide availability of Coors beer. "Sex can be dangerous, which is good for the marriage industry," van der Meer pointed out.

So what does all this mean for the future of weddings, and of the wedding industry? It is all very good news, apparently.

"The Echo Boom do their homework there, as well," she said. "They are traditional, but traditional doesn't mean old. They are doing things in a new way. They want the modern spin on traditions." She showed slides demonstrating the spin of tradition: the monogrammed aisle runner, red as a Hollywood carpet; the long dining table set with dozens of candles, like a votive altar in a baroque Neapolitan church, but without the stooped, black-clad grandmothers; the cute, shaggy pet dog garlanded with wreaths of flowers. "How can we feed into this? By creating weddings that people talk about," van der Meer said. And talk about weddings isn't just idle chat, she explained, but is itself a form of marketing. The Echo Boom bride will be surrounding herself with bridesmaids—an average of five per party—of whom it is estimated that three will, within the next year, become engaged themselves, and will therefore be looking for advice about how to stage their own neo-traditional events. "The bride is a powerful brand ambassador," van der Meer assured her audience.

Nina Lawrence, the publisher of *Brides*, had made some of the same points to me when we had lunch after the Wedding March on Madison: "Anyone who engages with this consumer is going to go for a nice ride" is how she had put it. But van der Meer was making a larger point about the Echo Boom bride and the generation to which she belonged. The Echo Boom generation, van der Meer said, "is already impacting our country as significantly as Boomers did." By that she didn't mean that the Echo Boomers were trying, as their parents had done with anti–Vietnam War rallies and feminist consciousness-raisings and civil rights agitation, to change the political culture of the country. Nor did she mean that Echo Boomers were engaged in the kind of sometimes indulgent therapeutic self-examination that so characterized their parents' early adult years.

What she was talking about, rather, was the Echo Boom's impact upon the commercial marketplace, and the social ramifications of that impact. For them, minivans had been invented—the first time an entire type of car had been created with kids' needs in mind. Toy stores had filled up their shelves with Cabbage Patch dolls, and had seen them empty over and over again. As teens, van der Meer said, the Echo Boom had fueled a billion dollars in annual sales of Mary-Kate and Ashley products, had driven the success of retailers like Old Navy and Abercrombie & Fitch, and had provided the impetus for the launch of AOL Instant Messenger, *Cosmogirl!*, *Teen Newsweek*, and *Teen People*. What she was saying was that the social transformation brought about by the Echo Boom was the creation of an ever more complex consumer marketplace and an ever more sophisticated consumer.

What van der Meer didn't address in her presentation, though, were the wider cultural implications of the emergence of this new, tradition-spinning bride—the implications beyond her immediate impact upon those who were in the business of providing her with goods and services. What did it mean, I wondered as I listened to her, that today's young woman—who has, by law, as much right as her male peers to education, to employment opportunity, to financial self-sufficiency, to political independence, and to the expression of sexual freedom— should want, on her wedding day, to affect the styles and manners of prefeminist femininity? And what kind of freedom was, in fact, hers to enjoy, that demanded in its name such scrupulous attention to her looks, her body, and her purchases?

I belong to Generation X, the demographic cohort that followed the Baby Boomers, and so while I don't remember firsthand the feminist campaigns of the sixties and seventies, I did grow up with a consciousness of enjoying the results of legal and social victories recently won. The Echo Boom bride, on the other hand, was born into a world in which those victories were well established, and is coming of age in a culture that promises that her enjoyment of social equality is not incompatible with feminine pursuits of the sort from which her mother's generation sought to be liberated.

The difference, or so the Echo Boom bride believes, is that when she assumes those trappings of prefeminist femininity, she is doing so for herself, not because anyone else has told her she must. One vivid instance of this is the public stripping by the groom of the bride's garter—a practice that, for many women immediately influenced by the achievements of feminism, as well as those who simply prefer not to have their own embarrassment written into the wedding-day schedule in advance, seems demeaning and undesirable: "Garters are practically obsolete," observed the *New York Times* in 1996. But latterly the practice has been reclaimed as a postfeminist piece of fun, with the manufacturers of garters happy to supply the goods, often in packs of two: one to throw and one to keep. (A recent innovation for the thoughtful bride who wishes to surprise her husband with that which her skirts conceal, in spite of the familiarity that is typical of modern premarital relations, is the novelty garter: for the sports fan, an NFL-themed garter, decorated with his favorite team's insignia; for the hunter, a camouflage garter decorated with a trinket of a deer's head; for the soldier, a garter with a dog tag; and for the firefighter, a red satin garter decorated with maribou feathers and a hanging charm of a Dalmatian.)

When the Echo Boom bride wears the gown in which she can barely move, the veil behind which her smile, with teeth bleached to a photogenic whiteness, is temporarily concealed, and the feathered garter that tickles her thigh, she believes that it is an expression of her modernity that she has chosen to be traditional. She holds to this conviction even though, as the eternal return of the bride in white on the cover of the bridal magazines suggests, the wedding industry does not offer her much in the way of choice to do otherwise; and even though the idea that anyone can choose to be traditional—that tradition can be a matter of choice, rather than of obligatory social conformity—is not one that would have made much sense in that past to which the Echo Boom wedding mistily alludes.

.   .   .

What, then, of the Echo Boom bride's parents—the Baby Boomers whose own generational quest had been to overturn tradition? How did it come about that their legacy would be their daughters' embrace of the big white wedding?

One answer to this question is the proposition that the conservative principles and the consumer sophistication of the Echo Boomers were directly transmitted by their parents—who were, after all, the ones who buckled them into their five-point safety harnesses, and who paid for all those minivans and Cabbage Patch dolls and subscriptions to *Teen People* in the first place. Boomer parents are, in many cases, paying for their children's wedding expenses, too, even while the past practice of the bride's father covering the bills is in decline. (According to the 2006 Condé Nast American Wedding Study, only 30 percent of brides' parents now have sole responsibility for the wedding costs. Fifteen percent of couples have help from both sets of parents, while a third of couples claim to pay for everything themselves. Of course, offspring who pay for everything themselves may only be able to afford to do so because their parents have supported them through college and sometimes through impecunious early employment.) Perhaps age has brought to the Boomers a greater attachment than they might have anticipated to the trappings of tradition, particularly upon an occasion as sentimental as a wedding. Condé Nast's Echo Boom report says that 80 percent of Echo Boom brides will have their father give them away, and it's easy to imagine that fathers who, in their own youth, may have scorned the authority of the older generation, will be irresistibly moved by this expression of deference on the part of their own children.

But an additional explanation occurred to me at the Business of Brides conference, which was that the emergence of the big white Echo Boom wedding was not so much a repudiation of the feminist principles of the Boomer generation as it was a direct consequence of them. One of the things that feminism has freed women to do is to have careers and responsibilities that render them far too busy to plan weddings, for themselves or for their daughters. The working bride is hardly a new phenomenon; a report produced in 1958 for *Brides* noted that 70 percent of engaged women were employed, six out of ten of them in clerical positions. But most of those fifties brides would have had mothers or aunts who didn't work, and who would have handled the process of planning and producing a wedding, from the selecting of a caterer or a florist in the case of more affluent families to the baking of cakes and the arranging of flowers among those of more modest means.

Members of the current generation of mothers and aunts have, however, found themselves able to have careers as well as children; and consequently a vacuum of assistance has arisen, with wedding professionals rapidly emerging to fill it. Planning a wedding, like taking care of the elderly or supervising children, has ceased to be part of the interfamilial household work of women, and has become work that is done by paid employees. Weddings have become part of the service economy; and the provider of those services, including the wedding planners at the Business of Brides conference, have a vested interest in ensuring that the services they are providing do not diminish in value to themselves.

This isn't to suggest that individual wedding planners inflate the expenses of their clients to increase their own profits (although there are certainly those who do). Indeed, hiring a wedding planner may well be effective for the busy bride, who will save herself in time what she expends in her planner's percentage. But the very existence of professional wedding planners—and the expansion of their ranks—contributes to the furtherance of Bridezilla culture, in which more is never enough. Drafted to cope with the complexity of the modern wedding, the professional wedding planner is likely also to increase the complexity; and so things spiral upward. And so, just as the "bride from hell" is the inevitable result of a wedding culture that insists upon perfectionism, so the professional wedding planner who derides her is instrumental in generating that culture of perfectionism in the first place.

Long before there was an Association of Bridal Consultants to promote the notion that every bride could benefit from enlisting professional help in planning her wedding, the elite in America were drawing upon the assistance of etiquette experts and service contractors for the nuptial event. *The Steward's Handbook*, a volume published in 1893, gives detailed descriptions of the proper arrangement of tables and chairs in a ballroom for a wedding banquet, advises on the correct way to conduct a receiving line and showcase wedding gifts, and gives suggestions for appropriate floral displays and wedding-cake decorations, these last sounding rather as if they were conceived by Martha Stewart's great-grandmother, with sugar work "showing forth some Shakespearean love story; Tennysonian idyll; or groupings of historic scenes from the family history."

By the thirties, department stores had established bridal salons staffed by what were known as bridal secretaries, sometimes well-born women who functioned as advisers as well as vendeuses. The head of the bridal department at Lord & Taylor, one Kathleen Blackburn, not only designed most of the store's dresses but often was on hand at the wedding rehearsal and, in the case of the most important of the thousand clients she outfitted each year, the wedding itself. According to "Here Comes the Bride's Business," an article in *Independent Woman* from 1939, Blackburn once flew to Pittsburgh to press a wedding dress "for a fashionable bride whose superstitious servants refused to touch the sacred gown." She could also, in a pinch, "recreate a wedding bouquet or a bridal wreath at ten minutes' notice out of the remains of last night's center-piece."

Those were the days when grand weddings were the preserve of grand people; services such as those Kathleen Blackburn provided were reserved for members of the American upper class, among whom centerpieces and servants were a part of everyday life. One of the things today's wedding planners promise to supply to their clients is instruction in the graces and manners of Kathleen Blackburn's elite of yore, even when they belong to no such elite themselves. Wedding planners advise clients who have never had to compose anything more formal than an e-mail on the correct way to word an invitation ("People now invite you to 'witness their love'—I don't want to witness someone making love, thank you very much," one experienced wedding planner told me with revulsion), and they instruct a bride who has been affecting a fashionable slouch since she was a teenager in the art of walking down the aisle one slow, stately, erect footstep at a time, so that she and her gown move in concert, gliding like a ship's prow cutting through still water.

Because America's elite has always been porous, with its membership accessible to those who can afford to buy their way in, the new rich have always required the instructions of experts in how to behave like the old rich. (Kathleen Blackburn's clients would have included the daughters of new money as well as old, of Irish descent as well as Dutch.) The manners of the old rich—which is to say the former Wasp elite—still linger in the conduct of weddings, but a more significant influence today is that exercised by America's new aristocracy, the aristocracy of celebrity. What was once considered proper is less important than what is now considered fashionable, such as serving brightly colored Vitaminwater in mason jars at your reception, like the singer Jessica Simpson did. And because ordinary Americans know that Jessica Simpson was not born to her fame, but started out as an ordinary American, then brides who aspire to marry in the manner of Jessica Simpson, if on a smaller budget—her ceremony and reception decorations required thirty thousand blushing white roses, and her diamond engagement ring–wedding ring combo totaled 6.75 carats—do so not because Simpson's success seems impossibly distant but because she seems, on the contrary, only a more successful version of themselves, even if her fabulous wedding was ultimately followed by divorce.

The wedding planners who service celebrities—the Kathleen Blackburns of today—are something close to celebrities themselves: Mindy Weiss, the Hollywood event planner who helped Jessica Simpson realize her nuptial vision became widely known among the reality-television-watching public when she arranged the wedding of Trista Rehn and Ryan Sutter, who had met on the show *The Bachelorette,* and whose wedding was subsequently broadcast by ABC over three nights, like the kind of interminable feasting-and-wassailing marathons undertaken at the marriages of medieval royalty, only with frequent commercial interruptions. (The final episode, in which Rehn and Sutter were actually married, was watched by 17 million Americans.) Some celebrities even have what you might call house wedding planners: Jennifer Lopez hired a wedding planner called Sharon Sacks for her second wedding, to Cris Judd, a dancer, in September 2001; having split from Judd, she also hired Sacks two years later, during her engagement to Ben Affleck, to plan a wedding that was canceled just days before it was due to take place. Preston Bailey, the wedding planner who showcased his floral cow at the Wedding March on Madison, is best known for planning the nuptials of Liza Minnelli and David Gest, the concert promoter, at which Elizabeth Taylor served as matron of honor; and for the wedding he designed for Melissa Rivers, the daughter of Joan Rivers, at the Plaza hotel in New York, which was inspired by the St. Petersburg of imperial Russia and for which he decorated the hotel's ballroom with scores of silver birch trees and thousands of white roses.

Weddings like those tend to lodge in the public imagination, and not just for the confirmation they provide—upon news of later divorce—that a spectacular wedding does not guarantee subsequent marital happiness. To join the ranks of these high-end event designers, and to become a handmaiden to celebrity clients, may not be the hope of all the would-be wedding planners who attend the Association of Bridal Consultants' annual conference, or who go to one of the many training seminars that it holds around the country the rest of the year, though it certainly is the aspiration of some. What those journeyman wedding planners do depend upon, though, is the furtherance of a wedding culture in which every bride is encouraged to imagine herself a celebrity for a day.

It has become a nuptial commonplace to think of a wedding as a star vehicle, with the bride the star in question, even when the reality of her circumstances is far distant from the world of the rich and famous. Through the Association of Bridal Consultants I met one would-be wedding planner who provided ample testimony to this fact. She was an African American legal assistant, and had grown up in the projects in Brooklyn, New York, but the economic limitation with which she and her peers had been raised did not diminish their hopes for a superlative wedding day. She told me she had helped with the wedding of a cousin who, having seen pictures of Melissa Rivers's wedding, decided that she, too, wanted to get married in a confected winter wonderland. The budget for this wedding reception was just two hundred dollars, compared with the 3 million that Rivers's reportedly cost.

"I went to the dollar store and I bought lots of little white lights left over from Christmas," the planner from Brooklyn told me. She floated votive candles in bowls for centerpieces, used ferns instead of floral decorations, and decorated the barren community hall in which the reception was taking place with white tulle, white balloons, and white branches. "It wasn't what Joan Rivers's daughter had, but it was nice," she said. The only bad part, she explained, was when the bride was obliged to open the cash gift envelopes she had been given in order to pay the DJ.

I heard this story—an extreme example of the widespread bridal experience whereby the desire to enact one's fantasies has the less than gratifying result of bankrupting one's purse—as the Brooklyn planner and I were riding home together on a train to New York City from Norwalk, Connecticut, where we had attended a seminar for novice wedding planners conducted by Jerry and Eileen Monaghan some weeks after the Kansas City conference. There were eighteen would-be consultants at the class, which took place in a conference room at a Doubletree hotel on a frigid winter's day. They were all women, ranged in age from twenties to fifties, and more than half of them were African American or Latina. Tracy, a consultant for Mary Kay cosmetics, confidently stated her intention to become what the Monaghans refer to as a Master Bridal Consultant—their top professional rank—within six years. Sarah had left law school in order to become an event planner: "Like the movie said, if you can't wed, plan," she said, a reference to *The Wedding Planner*, a romantic comedy from 2001 that starred Jennifer Lopez as a wedding consultant and gave the trade a boost in public recognition, even if the verisimilitude left rather a lot to be desired. (Lopez wore high heels throughout, and ended up marrying the fiancé of one of her clients.) Others, when asked by Jerry Monaghan to explain their reason for attending, had vaguer contributions to make: "I have just become interested, very interested in weddings, and things like that," said one young woman named Jennifer, limply.

The Monaghans worked a kind of good-cop, bad-cop routine, with Eileen adopting a more nurturing pedagogical style to that of her brusquer husband. Eileen provided hands-on, practical advice about conceptualizing a nascent wedding-planning business. What difference would it make if you called your business "Budget Brides" or "Elegant Affairs"? Should you acquire a business telephone number with a Manhattan area code even if the center of operations is actually your spare bedroom in Hackensack, New Jersey? She pointed out the pros and cons of receiving clients at home—the ability to create your own persuasively bridal atmosphere, with candles or flowers—or making house calls. "We had one consultant who always went to the bride's house, and the minute she drove up to the house she knew what the budget was going to be," she explained.

She compiled, with contribution from the room, a list of about two dozen items that, she said, every newly engaged woman needs help with. "There's the budget," she said. "The location. The time-line. The flowers. The decorations. The rentals. The paper. The music. The entertainment—you might include the clown that you need to keep the kids amused. There's the catering, the hotels, the negotiation, the photography, the videography, the favors, the personal care—that's hair, makeup, pedicure, and manicure. There's the site coordination, the transportation. There are the other parties: the rehearsal, the Sunday morning brunch, the bridesmaids' luncheon, the showers. There's the attire: You can deal with the tux company yourself and get a hundred percent markup. There's the honeymoon. The legal stuff: the prenup and the marriage license. There's the officiant. Organizing the bridal party. Etiquette. Gifts." Forty-three different businesses are involved in staging today's standard wedding, according to Eileen's list, which extended down two columns of the whiteboard that was set up at the front of the room, the scrawl of necessities filling the shining space.

When it was his turn to speak, Jerry Monaghan addressed the group in the breezily confrontational style of a television infomercial host. "Why are you in business? To make money," he said, answering his own question before any of his listeners had a chance to. Once a bride has shown any interest in hiring a consultant, he said, persistent follow-up was called for. "A letter, a phone call, send a thank-you note, a brochure—have your marketing plan in place, and hit them, and hit them again until they buy from you," he said. He recommended money-spinning add-ons to wedding consulting, suggesting that consultants sell invitations on which they could earn a 50 percent markup as well as leveraging brides into ordering announcement cards or personalized notepaper. He suggested that consultants should present themselves as wedding experts to feature editors at local newspapers, and they should attend bridal shows to promote themselves directly to the bride, adorning their booths with letters of recommendation from satisfied customers accompanied by photographs of smiling brides in full regalia. "Do they have to be the same person?" he said. "No. The best writers of letters are probably the less attractive brides. You want a lovely bride who can spell."

The most important thing, Jerry said, was to make the bride feel that hiring a wedding consultant wasn't a luxury but a necessity, at least if she wanted to have a wedding day she could actually enjoy. "Part of your marketing to brides is to say: Sure, you can do this yourself, but do you want to?" he said. "Do you have the two hundred hours it takes to plan your own wedding? You can change your own oil, but do you want to do that? Why do you take your car to the gas station to change your oil? Because the guy doing it is a professional." He recommended that consultants offer their own seminars on "How to Plan Your Own Wedding" to newly engaged women, and when the seminar participants looked puzzled at the suggestion, he grinned. "Why would you want to teach a bride to plan her own wedding?" he asked. "Because she's going to come out of the course going, 'Oh, God, I don't want to do all that.' We had one member who deliberately scared the brides to death this way, but you don't have to do that. Just show her what it involves and she'll be scared to death anyway."

Jerry recommended that his listeners adopt the salesman's bluster in their dealing with brides, and it seemed to me that he was using more than a little of that bluster himself. The health of his own association depends on persuading more and more novice wedding planners to sign up and on increasing the public acceptance of the notion that the services of professional wedding planners are not just for the rich, but for everybody. Monaghan, like the Condé Nast Bridal Group, benefits from a perception that the American wedding can only get bigger and more lavish, and while he was careful to warn his listeners of the hazards of starting up a new small business—he said that 50 percent of the new businesses founded each year in the United States didn't last longer than eighteen months, and 80 percent were shuttered within five years—his listeners still seemed to be struck by the allure of the career.

"Just because people don't have a lot doesn't mean they shouldn't have something nice," the planner from Brooklyn said to me about the low-budget weddings of her friends as we rode home from the seminar. She was right, of course; and the ingenuity of her effort to emulate Preston Bailey on a two-hundred-dollar budget was impressive. But it was hard to hear her describe the economic pressures on the brides she knew without feeling that Bridezilla culture was at work here, too—not only influencing the hopes and wishes of brides but also influencing the hopes and wishes of these women who sought to become professional wedding planners. Hosting a wedding that costs more than one can afford is nothing new among working-class Americans: An article published in *Suburban Life* magazine in 1912, called "The Evil of Elaborate and Showy Weddings," argued that wedding excess prevailed not only among the upper middle classes but also among the poor, who, the article reported, "are quick to follow the example set to them by their more fortunate neighbors. At their pitifully cheap festivities, they squander their hard-won earnings." Oversized gestures of hospitality by those with limited resources have long bewildered those more affluent who fail to understand that the urge to celebrate, and the urge to display one's capacity for largess, exists among the poor as well as the rich. The Brooklyn planner told me that her friends felt they had to give their guests wedding favors because they didn't want their guests to think they couldn't afford to do so. The fact that they couldn't afford to do so was an unfortunate reality that would be felt after the party was over, when the next rent check or grocery bill was due.

What was really striking was that the field once dominated by the likes of Kathleen Blackburn, the formidable overseer of the Lord & Taylor bridal department, should now have room for the aspirations of the women at the Association of Bridal Consultants seminar, who came from cultures and classes among which, not long ago, the idea of hiring a professional to help plan a wedding would have been unthinkable. The odds may have been heavily stacked against their professional success—just how the planner from Brooklyn would cover her costs, let alone make a living, planning weddings with budgets of two hundred dollars, was far from clear—but the hope was there. Just as the American bride has come to believe that the manners and customs of the celebrity class can be hers to enjoy, so all manner of Americans have been seized with the hope of participating in this new democracy of extravagance.

Jerry Monaghan told his "bride from hell" piñata anecdote at the Norwalk class as a cautionary tale for any of his listeners who might be contemplating essaying a career in the wedding industry because they were in love with the romance of weddings and with the iconic drama of the bride. The realities of the job, he was suggesting, are very different. And different they are.

But he told another favorite story, one that seemed to speak not just to the hopes of the brides, but to the hopes of those who sought to serve them. He described one successful member of the association, the late Dorothy Penner, a consultant from Louisville, Kentucky, in whose honor the association now gives an award every year.

"Miss Dorothy would never quote a fee," he said. "She would always say, 'Don't worry about money, we'll talk later.' Then she would sit down with the family the day after the wedding and say, 'Well, how much was that worth to you?'

"Miss Dorothy drove a Mercedes," Monaghan continued. "She got them in the afterglow, when everything was perfect. If you can get inside the bride's head, if you can dream what she is dreaming, you are no longer a worker charging an hourly rate. You are selling dreams, and you can charge anything."

It was good advice, if you want to be a successful salesperson: that the way to appeal to brides is through their most cherished wedding fantasies. But Monaghan was selling dreams to his class of would-be wedding planners, too: the dream of each that there might be room in this business of brides for one more wedding planner who could turn brides into clients and clients into stars.

Three

Inventing the Traditionalesque

The concept of tradition is an important one—and a vexed one—to the wedding industry. On the one hand, the industry leans heavily upon notions of tradition in marketing its products and services. On the other, it urges brides to think of tradition not according to its dictionary definition, as consisting of practices that are handed down from generation to generation, but as a kind of historical grab bag, a set of charming antique practices from which the bride might select those that best suit her tastes. There's nothing very traditional, after all, about an ordinary, middle-class American couple having a wedding that requires the services of forty-three different businesses for its preparation and staging, as well as the services of a professional to manage them—not, that is, if one's definition of tradition is to adhere to practices observed by earlier generations, rather than to adopt a few retro flourishes.

Today's bride might be surprised to learn just how many of the elements of a wedding she thinks of as traditional are, in fact, relative novelties, at least when it comes to the standard accoutrements of a middle-class, middle-American wedding. An article published in the *American Sociological Review* in 1939, entitled "The Cost of Weddings," by B. F. Timmons, a sociology professor at the University of Illinois, gives some indication of what were considered the basic requirements for a wedding in pre–World War II America among ordinary citizens (rather than among the elite clients of Kathleen Blackburn, at whom the new magazine *So You're Going to Be Married* and its advertisements from the burgeoning bridal industry were aimed). A third of Timmons's brides managed to do without an engagement ring, and 16 percent were married in clothes they already owned, rather than in a bridal gown or other new outfit. A third of the couples married without a wedding reception in addition to the ceremony, and about a third skipped the honeymoon or other postwedding trip, as well. The average cost of a wedding among Timmons's survey respondents was $392.30, which in 2006 would have a purchasing power of $5,700.

The traditions of *not* having an engagement ring or a bridal gown or a wedding reception or a honeymoon are those that the wedding industry has been more than happy to see wither away in the seventy years since Timmons's survey was conducted. The industry's definition of a traditional bride is one who embraces the trappings of Bridezilla culture with enthusiasm, and her less enthusiastic counterpart is, understandably, a problem. When *Vows* magazine, a trade publication for wedding-dress retailers, featured an article on catering to the "non-traditional bride," it noted that such customers "don't always make 'good' brides because they're often uncomfortable starring in the role of 'girl in a big white dress' " and warned retailers that the nontraditional bride was dangerously apt "to forget the wedding and prepare for marriage."

However promising this tendency might be for the bride's future marital prospects, it does not serve the interests of the person selling her a gown.

The wedding industry has been assiduous in working to establish the trappings of the lavish formal wedding as if they were compulsory rather than optional. One of the most vivid instances of the wedding industry inventing a tradition—the phrase derives from a celebrated essay by Eric Hobsbawm, the Marxist historian—is the positioning of a diamond engagement ring as an essential piece of matrimonial equipage. Americans started giving and wearing diamond engagement rings in the latter part of the nineteenth century, after the discovery of diamond mines in South Africa made the stones much more easily available than they had been hitherto. But it was in the 1930s that the advertising agency N. W. Ayer began to create on behalf of the De Beers diamond company a decades-long advertising and public-relations campaign to convince the American consumer that a diamond ring was an indispensable token of romantic love's measure. Crowning N. W. Ayer's achievement was a phrase coined in 1947 by a copywriter named Frances Gerety that *Advertising Age* magazine was later to call the best advertising slogan of the twentieth century: "A Diamond Is Forever."

Thanks to the efforts of Gerety—who never herself married—the imperative for a diamond engagement ring is today so well established that current De Beers's marketing campaigns have focused not simply upon the necessity of a diamond, but the necessity of a really, really big diamond. (One recent advertisement shows a large stone and a smaller one side by side, the caption under the smaller reading, "Where'd you get that diamond?" and the caption under the larger reading, "Where'd you get that man?") The convention that a man should spend two months' salary on his bride's ring was also created by the jewelry industry, and the De Beers Web site, adiamondisforever.com, provides a handy calculator for figuring out two months' salary from an annual wage, helpful for any would-be groom who can't divide by six. (Where'd you get that man, indeed.)

All traditions are invented, in the sense that they are the product of culture rather than nature; and just because a so-called tradition arises from commercial imperatives rather than being an organic expression of pre-industrial folk culture—which is the place we tend to think of traditions coming from—does not diminish its hold on the popular imagination. Diamond engagement rings are now traditional, even if the tradition originated in the economic interests of diamond companies. But what is distinctive about contemporary weddings is not just that the industry itself sets out to establish traditions; it is that the American bride and groom are invited to invent and establish new traditions for themselves. Thus a company called Mary's Kreations can offer as a wedding-day trinket a pewter disk imprinted with one of a range of images appropriate to participants in a wedding (a basket of flowers for a flower girl, a cushion for a ring bearer) called the Heirloom Ornament—even though the very definition of an heirloom is something that is passed down through the generations, not bought over the counter at a bridal store. Mary, whoever she may be, is undoubtedly hoping that her buyers will overlook that inconvenient fact, so that—rather than her Heirloom Ornaments actually being handed down as heirlooms—future generations will purchase her Kreations anew.

The idea that couples can invent tradition on a personal level is a much shakier proposition than the notion of tradition being invented on a culturewide level, as with the work of N. W. Ayer for De Beers—for in what sense can anything be said to be traditional if it neither has been observed in the past nor is certain to be observed in the future? It is not impossible that the as yet unborn daughters of Echo Boom brides will seek to emulate their mothers' choices, but a practice does not become a tradition until it has gained historical and cultural traction, and whether garlanded pets as wedding attendants will achieve that status remains to be seen.

What is marketed as tradition by the wedding industry could better be called the *traditionalesque*—a pleasing mélange of apparently old-fashioned, certainly nostalgic, intermittently ethnically authentic practices that may have little relevance to the past or to the future and are really only illustrative of the present in which they emerge. *Tradition* is one of those words, like *homeland* or *motherhood*, that is most frequently invoked when what it represents is under threat, or is in abeyance; and the emphasis placed upon the notion of tradition by the wedding industry points to a contradiction at the industry's core: The imperative of economic expansion demands the introduction of new services and new products, but those products and services must be positioned not as novelties but as expressions of enduring values. (Hence the inclusion of a pet dog in a wedding ceremony is positioned as an expansion of the definition of family.) This tension—between the restless invention of the new and the yearning for the solidity of the established—is at the core not just of the wedding industry, but also of the larger American culture of which it is a part. We want the new to seem old, and the old to seem reassuringly new.

Montecito, in Southern California, is one of those blessed towns in which the natural beauty of the location—the Santa Barbara mountains lying behind, the Pacific Ocean before—has combined with the unnatural prosperity of the residents to create an American idyll. Architect-designed homes are concealed behind landscaped hedges. Luxury cars purr down leafy roads that are immaculately maintained. Oprah Winfrey has a house there, for which she paid $50 million, and Ty Warner, the billionaire inventor of Beanie Babies, owns the Four Seasons hotel. Montecito isn't the kind of place you come to to make money: The only strivers are the gardeners and maids who keep it looking so beautiful, and who, in any case, live in the less affluent districts of Santa Barbara. Montecito is the kind of place you come to when it's time to turn the money you've made into material comforts and environmental pleasures, into French granite countertops and multimillion-dollar ocean views.

One of Montecito's inhabitants is Beverly Clark, whose name, while less recognizable to Americans at large than those of some of her neighbors, is as recognizable within the wedding industry as is Oprah Winfrey's beyond it. Clark and her husband, Nelson Clark, run Beverly Clark Enterprises, through which they produce a variety of wedding-related goods and services. There is the Beverly Clark Collection, a range of wedding accessories that is sold in bridal stores. There is *Planning a Wedding to Remember,* a bestselling book. The Clarks own a number of Web sites, including weddinglocation .com and honeymoonlocation.com, that market hotels to marrying couples (barmitzvahlocation.com belongs to the Clarks, too). The Clarks have served as consultants to companies seeking to appeal to the wedding market, ranging from the Marriott hotel chain, for which they developed a training program for managers, to the Bank of America, which sought Beverly out when promoting home equity loans as a source of wedding funding.

I wanted to meet Beverly Clark because I had been amazed, as I read through bridal magazines and paged through wedding-industry trade publications, by the proliferating volume of stuff that is produced for the wedding market: the resin coach-shaped favors that open like treasure boxes; the heart-shaped cookie-cutter favors, with cookie recipe included; the Eloquence Sterling Handle Kissing Bell, to be rung during the bride and groom's embrace at the reception; floral-painted toasting flutes; Sweet Passion–scented wardrobe sachets shaped like sexy lace-up corsets; Wedding Sprinkles flower-seed tins; Celebrate Romance Surprise Balls containing charms, gems, and shells; plates printed with hearts, doves, flowers, and bells; candles with silver-ball toppings and a wedding cake fragrance; personalized confetti available in a festive combination of colors and motifs; bread-dough ornaments that can be used as cake-toppers and then turned into decorations for the Christmas tree; scratch-off save-the-date cards, on which the wedding date is temporarily concealed by three hearts; and the Woodstock Wedding Chime featuring Johann Pachelbel's "Canon in D."

No bride incorporates all of these different *objets* into her wedding, and many brides will find none of the above to her taste. But every bride is the object of the wedding industry's insistence that purchasing the products it offers amounts to the observance of valuable tradition. "There are 2.3 million reasons when you hear wedding bells ringing these days why you should also hear cash registers ringing" is how one article in *Gifts & Decorative Accessories* magazine addressed its readership of retailers. "Certain things are part of every wedding—wedding invitations, thank-you notes, cake boxes, cake toppers, cake knives and servers, toasting goblets, pens, gifts, and guest registry books, file boxes, favors, and attendants' gifts. . . . You are dealing with sentiment; that has no price tag." Nelson Clark, who is known as Herk, was shortly to tell me something very similar: "One of the first guys who ever put our product into his stores once told me, 'Let me tell you something, son. There are three occasions, a birth, a wedding, and a death, when people spend more money. And I get as much as I can in those situations.' "

The Beverly Clark Collection alone offers more than eight hundred different quasi-traditional products, from cake servers with silk flowers attached to the handle to guest books decorated with pearls and lace to embroidered handkerchiefs for the mother and grandmother of the bride; and I hoped that the Clarks might help me understand how this plethora of product had become part of the American wedding. When I arrived at the Clarks' house—which, in an exemplary expression of the traditionalesque, was modeled upon a French chateau, in warm yellow stone with a slate roof, its three-car garage disguised as an elegant stables building—Beverly was standing in the hall, which had marble floors, a sweeping staircase, and, at the bottom of the banister, an enormous urn of flowers. She was petite and pretty, with blond hair and blue eyes and smooth cheeks that had been carefully protected against the sun's harsh rays. She was unpretentious and warm in manner, immediately taking me on a tour of her home as if she were a very well brought up little girl who, when introduced to a new playmate, shares her toys without being told to do so.

The house was decorated in a style favored by conservative wealth in California: Different periods of European history were referenced and blended into one luxurious, contemporary whole. "I love froufrou," Beverly said as she showed me the dining room, which had a table so highly polished that it appeared to be made from marble, and antique chairs, the provenance of which Beverly was uncertain about but which she thought were Louis Quatorze. "My husband says, 'If you bring back one more gold chair . . . ,'" she said, with a conspiratorial air. A panel of drapery on the ceiling looked like it was a style tip picked up from Versailles, but was only a disguise for the embedded loudspeakers. The kitchen had rustic-looking ceramic tiles and stenciled patterns on the flue over the stove, and there was a breakfast nook with a chandelier over which ivy artfully clambered. At the other end of the house was a family room, with dark wooden paneling and leather couches and a pool table. "We wanted it to feel like a European hotel," said Beverly, and the Clarks had done an impressive job of bringing a hint of a chilly northern latitude to their bright corner of paradise. The sitting room, meanwhile, was decorated like a very fancy dollhouse, with a white carpet, plump upholstery, delicate gilt chairs, heavy swag curtains, and side tables swathed in rich, oversized tablecloths and set with silver picture frames. At the foot of a couch there was, as a decorative item, a pair of lace-up Victorian-style ankle boots, as if the lady of the house had just come in from the very pretty garden that could be seen through the windows and was curled up on the couch having her tender toes massaged by a doting, frock-coated husband.

Beverly and Herk took me to lunch at the country club to which they belong, the Coral Casino, which Ty Warner, the Beanie Babies mogul, had just acquired. Café tables were set around a brilliant blue swimming pool, which, on account of the building's favorable position on the shore, appeared to vanish into the similarly brilliant blue ocean. They had gone into the wedding business, they explained, after Beverly had planned their own wedding, which took place in 1984 not far away from where we were sitting.

"When I look back at it now, it looks just like a normal wedding," said Beverly, who was wearing enormous sunglasses with ink-black lenses. "But this was right at the time when people were starting to choose alternative sites for weddings. My husband always had a vision of getting married at the beach, being a surfer from Malibu, but I was from Santa Barbara, and I wanted to have something a little more formal. I wasn't ready for the sand."

Herk looked down at his Cobb salad in mock-abashment.

"So I went to movie-location companies and found a house here in Montecito that was right on the cliff, with an ocean view and beautiful formal Italian European gardens," said Beverly.

"It was beautiful," agreed Herk.

"And another thing that we did that was still unusual at the time was to have food stations set up in different places," Beverly continued. "So it was not very formal, but very elegant."

"So people get up and move around, and there is that energy," added Herk.

"It looked like you were on a cruise ship," added Beverly. "It was a warm balmy night, which it never is here. And we had candles, and twinkle lights in the trees."

"Twenty years ago, twinkle lights in the trees was an oddity," said Herk. "Votive candles everywhere—that was an oddity."

"People have started to become more creative," said Beverly, thoughtfully. "Now it's like, 'That was a fun party.' Whereas before it was like, 'Oh, man, we're invited to this wedding.'"

After the wedding, Beverly's friends started to ask her to help plan theirs, and this led to the writing of *Planning a Wedding to Remember,* now in its seventh edition. Through the book, Herk explained, Beverly had a hand in establishing the popularity of a number of new wedding customs that have spawned small industries of their own. "Take the trend of having butterflies released at your wedding," he said. "When we first saw that, we put it in Bev's book, and there became a butterfly industry, so to speak. Then, when Kodak came out with their throwaway cameras, Bev wrote about the whole protocol of how you use a camera—how you get everybody up out of their seats so the energy is high at the wedding, and that became a whole industry. We were too dumb to capture it. Another idea was that Beverly used to tell people, get children's bubbles and wrap a beautiful label around them for your wedding day. And so a whole bubble industry was spawned." The lost bubble industry seemed to irk Herk.

In other instances, the Clarks had provided, through the Beverly Clark Collection, the products for the new traditions they were helping to establish. "We did a big push on picture-frame place cards," said Beverly. "We trademarked that name. The idea was to use little silver frames as a place card, and a favor."

"We trademarked the term 'Special touches and unique ideas,'" Herk said. "So everything we do has a special touch or a unique idea. Like when Beverly wrote in her book, 'Before you get to the altar, stop and take a rose out of the bouquet and hand it to your mother and say something to her.' Just touches like that."

As I listened to the Clarks describe their nuptial aesthetic—the rose handed to the mother by the bride; the picture-frame place cards, seven-dollar versions of the antique silver ones on display in their living room—I began to think about the historical referents to which they alluded. I also remembered the lace-up boots by the Clarks' couch. The touch of Victoriana was no accident: In the wedding industry, gestures toward the Victorian era—or, at least, toward a bastardized aesthetic derived from Victoriana and filtered through the lens of the romance novel and the Disney cartoon—are omnipresent; and the Clarks' quasi-traditionalism partook of these gestures, too. Much of what we now think of as nuptial tradition derives from Victorian models. The sentimentalizing of the bride as a mainstay of mass culture was, after all, a phenomenon of the nineteenth century, just as it is of our own time: The young Queen Victoria's wedding to her cousin Prince Albert, in 1840, was celebrated as a popular event to an unprecedented degree even for royal weddings, with coverage of her gown's manufacture in the *Times* (the labor of two hundred lace workers in the village of Honiton) and the bride's passage from St. James's Palace, where the marriage ceremony was conducted, to her residence at Buckingham Palace witnessed by multitudes of spectators.

The Victorian era was the last time that a crinoline and bustle amounted to contemporary fashion, and the modern-day fetish for ceremonial nuptial flatware—the beribboned cake-cutting knives and silver-plated servers—recalls the late-nineteenth-century mania for setting the table with outlandishly specific silver cutlery, so that pickles and strawberries could all be eaten with their own designated implements and a single place setting might require twenty-five different forks. Everyday decorative tastes in the Victorian era tended toward excess no less than do the maximalist urgings of the wedding industry today; and the modern bride who might prefer, in her regular life, the minimalism of Calvin Klein or Ikea, is easily persuaded on her wedding day to deck herself and her environs in the manner of an overstuffed Victorian drawing room.

The contemporary American wedding is far from Victorian in many aspects—consider the bachelorette party with male strippers—but the air of Victoriana provided by Beverly Clark, and by others of her ilk, supplies a sense of the historical and the traditional to brides and grooms whose immersion in modernity may otherwise be total. The enormity of the commitment required by marriage is a daunting thing, and it may be comforting to be reminded that generations have made it before—even if the modern contract of marriage, based upon equality of the partners, differs in drastic and fundamental ways from the contracts of the past. This is the function of the traditionalesque: to provide for the bride whose freedom has been bought at the expense of tradition the reassurance that her choices will be sustained by more than her will alone.

After lunch the Clarks and I returned to their home, where we sat in the wood-paneled family room and they told me about the other side of their business: supplying wedding-industry know-how to companies and corporations who sought to appeal to the bridal market. The hospitality industry, they explained, was beginning to realize how valuable these customers could be. "Like, if you are a hotel, and you can accommodate a horse and carriage, you should tell your future bride that you can accommodate a horse and carriage," Herk said. "Then she will start thinking about having a horse and carriage, and you can say to her, 'We have two people that offer that service; one of them has a white one.' But if you don't start getting the bride thinking, she's not going to think of it on her own. So that's what makes your property unique. You see: special touches and unique ideas."

One of the companies for which they had consulted, they told me, was Disney. In the mid-nineties Beverly had been on a Disney board of advisers, drawn from all over the wedding industry, that had given the company recommendations on how to appeal to the wedding market, a process Disney had begun by establishing a dedicated Fairy Tale Wedding department in 1991. "They had dress manufacturers and wedding magazine editors," she said. "We would get together for a long weekend and advise them about everything a bride wants and how they should market themselves." The results were impressive, according to Herk. "They started at zero, and they got up to a hundred million dollars a year on weddings," he said. I should go and take a look, the Clarks told me. And so, not long after visiting Montecito, I went to Walt Disney World in Orlando to see how wedding traditions were being invented there.

Cinderella's Coach was idling in the driveway when I approached the Wedding Pavilion at Walt Disney World. The coach, an orb-shaped plexiglass vehicle drawn by six white ponies, was manned by three footmen, who were wearing white wigs, ivory-colored frock coats, and gold lamé britches over white hose. It was a humid morning, like so many in Florida. "Those pants must be hot!" I said brightly to one of the footmen. Disney staff members who populate the theme parks in costume aren't ever supposed to break out of character when encountering the public, but this one couldn't resist. "They feel like they are stitched inside with fishing wire," he replied glumly.

I was at the Wedding Pavilion to meet with Korri McFann, a brand marketing manager for Disney who had been assigned to show me around, and as I was commiserating with the footman she emerged from Franck's Bridal Studio. This is the center of Disney's wedding-planning operations, where clients meet with Disney advisers to browse tables set with examples of the linens and china and flatware available for their receptions and gaze at inedible replicas of the wedding cakes available from Disney's confectioners, including one set with an enormous white-chocolate topper in the shape of the Cinderella Castle from the Magic Kingdom theme park. Franck's (it rhymes with "honks") feels less like a real bridal salon than like a Hollywood fantasy of a bridal salon—which is exactly what it is, having been modeled upon the establishment belonging to the persnickety wedding planner in the remake of *Father of the Bride*, a movie released by Touchstone, a Disney subsidiary.

McFann had immaculately applied makeup and eyes of such a vivid forest green that they looked as if they had been done with Technicolor, like those of a Disney cartoon character. "Certainly, the coach is very Cinderella, and nobody does Cinderella better than we do," she told me with a broad, unconvincing smile, as she firmly led me away from the footmen.

Cinderella's Coach, the rental of which costs twenty-five hundred dollars per ceremony, is one of the most coveted items available through Disney's Fairy Tale Weddings & Honeymoons program, but, as McFann explained as we sat in an office in Franck's, there are many other options available to brides and grooms who choose a Disney wedding. A Disney custom wedding, she said, might consist of anything from a ceremony under the gazebo at the Yacht Club, followed by a reception in a private banquet hall (converted from its daytime use as a conference room), to a wedding conducted in Disney's MGM Studios theme park, with the couple and guests cast as movie stars being mobbed by Disney employees enacting the roles of avid movie fans. An Intimate Wedding, on the other hand, presented a less extravagant possibility for couples who were prepared to limit their guest list to eighteen and to conform to a package deal that included the provision of a bouquet, boutonniere, cake, a bottle of champagne, and a violinist for the ceremony and reception.

McFann insisted that all the weddings were very tasteful, and while couples could draw upon Disney's storied back catalog if they so desired, the ceremonies themselves were, she explained, appropriately lacking in frivolity. Thus while employees playing Mickey and Minnie were available to make an appearance at a reception, at a cost of just over a thousand dollars for half an hour, any request to have Mickey attend a ceremony—or, for that matter, conduct one—would be politely declined. "We certainly pride ourselves that the ceremony is very traditional," McFann said earnestly—although, I was interested to learn, Disney's interpretation of tradition is flexible enough to permit an employee playing the role of Major Domo, Prince Charming's footman in the Disney version of *Cinderella*, to perform as a ring bearer. "He is in his full regalia with his costume and grand hat, and he has a velvet pillow with a glass slipper that sits on it," McFann said. "That is quite a moment. The guests love it. They have no idea that he is coming, and they certainly get into the spirit of that. He gives a lot of fairy-tale magic."

After we left Franck's, McFann led me to the Wedding Pavilion itself, which is reached by crossing a gated bridge to a man-made peninsula on the Seven Seas Lagoon, the swampy mere at the center of the Disney property. "We call this our crown jewel," McFann said as we entered the pavilion, which is built in a nineteenth-century, plantation-style architectural fashion, with white-painted wooden walls and a gray roof. It looks rather like something Queen Victoria might have enjoyed as a garden retreat at one of her palaces, though she would have made do without its state-of-the-art concealed videography and audio system. She would also have lacked the organ upon which, in addition to playing the usual processional and recessional choices, a Disney organist can perform "Someday My Prince Will Come" from *Snow White* or "When You Wish Upon a Star" from *Pinocchio*.

Inside there were comfortable pews, their ends carved in the shape of hearts, and French windows draped with diaphanous fabric, giving onto views of the water. Perfectly framed in the window at the head of the aisle was a view of the Cinderella Castle in the Magic Kingdom—a view which, McFann was quick to point out, is not obscured when the chuppah is erected for Jewish weddings. The pavilion was lofty and light and had the atmosphere of a church dedicated to a particularly approachable and unvengeful deity, one whose commandments might include "Thou shalt remember to floss."

The Wedding Pavilion opened for business in 1995, four years after Disney had established its Fairy Tale Weddings program, and its opening indicated Disney's realization that offering bridal traditionalism could be a very lucrative business. When the wedding program was first launched, the company's top executives had expected that the opportunity to get married within the environs of the Magic Kingdom would appeal primarily to hard-core Disneyphiles, and the early marketing was designed with those consumers in mind. (One advertisement for Disney weddings showed a bride and groom beaming at a Mickey impersonator.) There was, indeed, a market for such weddings, particularly among Japanese visitors, but before long the founders of the nascent Fairy Tale Weddings program began to realize that much more could be generated from the business of weddings than had hitherto been capitalized on. They established the advisory board upon which Beverly Clark sat, with the mission of generating ideas for top management—a management that was, Clark said, initially resistant to the idea of changing the marketing approach. "They kept wanting to put Mickey Mouse in their ads," Clark told me in Montecito. "We kept saying, 'You have done a great job with Mickey; people know you have Mickey; but what they don't know is that you can have this elaborate event there.' Everyone in the room was saying, 'Forget the mouse ears.'" The message got across, and rather than continuing to squeeze the wedding business in around existing Disney attractions—a quick ceremony with a handful of guests at most, followed by a photo session in front of the Cinderella Castle, was the extent of many of the early weddings—it was decided to invest in a wedding-specific infrastructure, including the Wedding Pavilion and Franck's.

"They were trying to increase the size of the wedding," Beverly Clark told me. "They could schedule weddings for two people every hour and a half, but they realized there were a lot of dollars in the reception, and that they had beautiful ballrooms and other activities they could offer." One year the advisory board members were witness, in a happy confluence of matrimonial joy and public-relations efficacy, to an actual wedding of the sort that the company hoped to promote: that of Rebecca Grinnals, one of the cofounders of the Fairy Tale Weddings program. The weekend-long celebration included a Western-themed rehearsal dinner at the Fort Wilderness resort, with line dancing and an appearance by Mickey and Minnie in farmers' outfits; a Mad Hatter's tea party/bridesmaids' luncheon; a ceremony at the Wedding Pavilion; a cocktail cruise; and a formal reception dinner at the Grand Floridian hotel concluding with a seventies-style disco.

The invention of tradition, or the traditionalesque, is the stock-in-trade of the Walt Disney Company, which has built upon the swampy nothingness of Florida an ersatz American heartland, with, at the center of the Magic Kingdom, a faux-Victorian Main Street filled with stores selling nothing but ice cream and branded souvenirs. Korri McFann had said that Disney prided itself upon its traditionalism when it came to weddings; but the traditions that are most determinedly upheld at Disney were those established by the company itself. Weddings are, for Disney, a very useful tool for attracting and keeping customers—a preoccupation of the company at any time, but especially at the time when the Wedding Pavilion opened. In the mid-nineties the number of visitors to Walt Disney World had been declining as the company's dominance in the entertainment-vacation industry was challenged by other destinations such as Las Vegas—which at the time was promoting itself as a family-friendly resort town—and Branson, Missouri, which offered live music, lakes, and golf. In November 1994 Judson Green, the president of Walt Disney Attractions, told *USA Today* that it was "getting harder and harder to find that traditional Disney family."

Disney realized that weddings provided an excellent means of addressing their problem. "Wedding couples are highly brand receptive in this stage of their lives," Rebecca Grinnals said in an online teleconference conducted on the Clarks' Web site weddinglocation.com for the benefit of hotel and catering managers, after she had left Disney to form her own consulting company. "Every decision they make has long-term implications. If you handle their wedding and their honeymoon correctly, you create cherished friends. . . . At Disney, we had couples return every single year to renew their vows. Talk about valuable, valuable lifelong guests." How better to reach Judson Green's "traditional Disney family" than to be there for the moment when a new family is created?

.   .   .

For insight into the tastes and desires of Disney brides—there have been more than twenty-five thousand of them since the weddings department was launched—I turned to the online message boards frequented by Disney-mooners, as they are known in company parlance. There, correspondents with screen names such as Tiggerbride and Eeyore1928 and Fantasia Sam trade tips on how to have a Disney wedding: where to buy Minnie Mouse bridal beanies, or whether to order as a dessert the Cinderella Slipper, a white chocolate shoe filled with three tiers of raspberries and whipped cream, set on a plate decorated with chocolate sauce that has been stamped with the impression of a castle. They also explain their choice of Disney as a wedding or honeymoon resort. "We chose WDW because, Why NOT!!" wrote one Disneymooner. "Is it not one of the most magical and wonderful places on the earth? I know that's where I would want to be for such a special occasion! When I fell in Love with my Fiancé, I had the same feeling I'd had when I was in WDW, which is a most wonderful and overwhelming feeling. It was a Happy feeling and I always told him that I'd feel as though I'd died and gone to heaven if I could be with him in WDW."

Disney's wedding offerings married the make-believe traditionalism of the Wedding Pavilion with an appeal to girlish fantasy—the Cinderella Coach—that seemed to resonate powerfully with the brides who had chosen to marry there. "We are naming our tables after Cinderella themed things, having Cinderella place cards, and bought plastic glass slippers and [are] cutting them to use as place card holders," wrote one bride on the planning boards. "We used Cinderella invitations and save the date cards, and will dance to a Disney song after the cake. . . . We also ordered a Cinderella unity candle, bought Cinderella and Prince toasting flutes . . . and ordered a Cinderella and Prince etched hurricane lamp for our table. . . . We are adding the touches of Disney without making it look too juvenile . . . or so we hope."

Whether there is any sense in which a Cinderella-themed wedding can be anything other than juvenile is a good question, but the larger fantasy that it draws upon—that every bride on her wedding day is a princess—is a widespread one. (It is also one emphatically encouraged by the wedding industry: As an instructor on a videotape for would-be wedding planners tells her listeners, "You will talk to one bride who says, 'No way am I going to spend that kind of money on my wedding,' and then you'll talk to somebody else who says, 'I am never going to do this again, it is a once-in-a-lifetime event, I am going to spend whatever it takes to get my dream wedding.' There are some brides who want the Cinderella picture, right down to the horse-drawn carriage that looks like a Cinderella carriage. That is the kind of client you want—ka-ching, ka-ching, ka-ching.") The fantasy is always that of being a princess rather than a queen, who enjoys a more distinguished, and potent, form of regality. But why should a wedding day be seized by brides as an opportunity for a flight into girlishness rather than—as a wedding day might alternately be characterized—an ascension into womanhood?

Perhaps, I considered at Walt Disney World, as I watched the bride and groom for whom the Cinderella Coach's footmen had been readying themselves climb aboard after their ceremony and ride away, this is the ultimate incarnation of the so-called traditional bride—the "girl in a big white dress," as *Vows* magazine described her—even if the traditions she is adhering to are ones established in cartoon versions of fairy tales and storybook versions of the lives of royalty. The contemporary American bride lives a life largely unfettered by the restrictions enforced in more traditional societies: She marries whomever she wants and maintains her independence after marriage. Such freedoms, though, come at the price of instability. It is, in many ways, harder to invent yourself than to have your course mapped out for you. And so the trappings of faux traditionalism—of the traditionalesque—provide the bride with the reassuring, if illusionary, sense that she does not stand alone at the daunting brink of marriage, but has all of history to lean upon.

Four

"The 'Oh, Mommy' Moment"

The Bridal Mall in Niantic, Connecticut, can be a very busy place on a Saturday afternoon. Young women occupy the dressing rooms at the rear of the store, stepping carefully into gowns that are the size of pup tents. Members of the sales staff bustle about, pulling gowns from the racks where they hang in plastic covers like chrysalides mid-metamorphosis, and, when a bride emerges from a dressing room to evaluate her fantastical makeover, offering veils and tiaras to complete the picture. One Saturday at the Bridal Mall, I watched as a twenty-eight-year-old music teacher whose wedding was less than four months away and who was shopping with her mother in tow, tried on half a dozen dresses. The last had a scooped, off-the-shoulder neckline and a full skirt and was decorated with white flowers. When the music teacher put it on, she suddenly looked dreamy-eyed and started smoothing the front of her skirt with her hands as if she were stroking the flank of a star-tled horse to calm it. "This is the one that will make him forget to breathe," she said.

The white wedding gown is the paramount icon of the American wedding—the pristine, untouched costume in which a bride makes her breathtaking appearance before her husband-to-be, as utterly transformed from her day-to-day self as is the butterfly emerging from its chrysalis. I had gone to the Bridal Mall—which is the largest independent bridal store in Connecticut, offering about eight hundred different styles—in an attempt to find out where wedding dresses come from: to trace the backstory of this object that seems, when it is worn for the first and only time, conjured into existence, with an air of the mythical about it, as if endowed with magical powers. I hoped that by exploring the world of bridal gowns—the wedding-industry product nonpareil—I might gain some insight into the pressures and preoc-cupations of those who depend upon the so-called traditional bride for a liv-ing: for whom, like the staff at the Bridal Mall, each sale is a reason for rejoicing. (When a consultant at the Bridal Mall closes a deal with a bride, she rushes out of the dressing area toward her colleagues clustered at the checkout counter, holding up three fingers above her head in the shape of a W for "win"; a failed sales pitch ends in a sorry L-shaped hand gesture, for "lose.") But I also hoped that by looking into the business of bridal gowns I might better understand how the mystique of this object—which is, after all, only a dress—is so powerfully maintained, so that each bride who wears it is enraptured and enraptures. This was a project that would eventually take me all the way from Connecticut to a factory floor in southern China, where, I was to discover, bridal rapture was a commodity in limited supply.

What the music teacher experienced as she tried on her final dress was something I had heard described at a training seminar for bridal retailers some months earlier as "the 'Oh, Mommy' moment"—an apt expression for the instant in which the music teacher felt not as if she were choosing her dress, but as if her dress were choosing her. Wedding magazines counsel brides to expect this you'll-know-it-when-you-see-it sensation, and bridal stores trade upon it, too: Kleinfeld, the storied New York wedding-dress emporium, greets women who make an appointment with a letter announcing, "We believe the day you choose your wedding gown should be as joyful and memorable as the day you wear it." (The wedding-industry rhetoric that insists a bride will just *know* when she's found the One—the one dress, that is—reminds me of teen-magazine advice pages counseling the worried reader who is not sure if she's experienced orgasm: If you have to ask, you haven't.) "The 'Oh, Mommy,' moment" may not, in fact, be universal—the number of brides on eBay seeking to sell their first-acquired gown, having later found another one they prefer—is testament to the influence of whim over commitment. But the idea that for each bride there is an ideal dress waiting to be found, as in the Aristophanic myth of separated lovers in Plato's *Symposium*, is a powerful one, and one that owners of bridal stores like the Bridal Mall are well advised to capitalize on.

This, at least, was the message of the seminar at which I learned about "the 'Oh, Mommy' moment," which took place in Las Vegas at the North American Bridal Association's semiannual meeting, a trade show for wedding-dress retailers and manufacturers. The seminar was entitled "Winning Bridal Strategies" and was delivered at the New York-New York hotel by Chip Eichelberger, a motivational speaker based in Tennessee, who got his start on the speaking circuit by working for Anthony Robbins, the bestselling author of *Awaken the Giant Within*.

"I am excited to be here, and I am challenged to be here," Eichelberger announced as he strode to the podium in a conference room that was filled with about seventy bridal-store owners, and kicked things off by asking the members of the audience to give their nearest neighbor a back rub. (I found myself being worked over by the hands of a burly retailer from Atlanta.) He then launched into a peppy exhortation filled with attention-getting, counterintuitive statements. "People say you should satisfy the customer, but setting out to satisfy the bride is a losing game," he said. The bridal-store owners looked puzzled. "Satisfaction is mediocrity," Eichelberger continued. "If you set the bar at satisfaction, some people on your team will set out to satisfy. You have to set up a system to exceed expectations. You've got to think, How can I provide a better experience for the bride?"

If Eichelberger's listeners were expecting dazzling insight from a specialist in the business of brides, they were probably disappointed: Weddings were not his area of expertise, and the tips he offered were rudimentary principles of salesmanship translated to the bridal context. Even so, it was enlightening to hear how Eichelberger instructed his listeners to pay attention to the emotional dimensions of the sale—a recommendation very familiar in today's sales lexicon, but all the more pertinent when the purchase is one already so charged with emotion.

"Some salespeople start at the lower end instead of the high end," he said. "If you get them excited about the three-hundred-dollar dress, it's hard to get them excited about the thousand-dollar dress." A bride's anxiety—about her dress, about her mother-in-law, even about the man she is marrying— should be greeted as providing an opening for the self-assured salesperson. "A lot of people are scared going into marriage, and if you can transfer your certainty, that's good for you," Eichelberger said. Stores should send e-mails to brides who came to browse but had yet to buy—"There's a difference between being pushy and following up," he said—and they should consider traditional seduction techniques. "After the weekend is over, hire some kid with a bike for eight dollars an hour and have him ride around and deliver a single rose to everyone who placed an order," he said. "There is nothing wrong with inducing a little reciprocation, if it is done elegantly. I would wager that's why a lot of brides buy from a salon: because the consultant spent so much time with them. You have to help them buy what they really want, not what they need."

And then there was "the 'Oh, Mommy' moment." "When the bride comes out of the dressing room and looks at herself in the mirror and says, 'Oh, Mommy,' you need to say, 'Let's write it up,'" Eichelberger said. "You owe it to them. Do they really want to go to nine other appointments at nine other stores? Of course they don't. You're cheating them if you don't say it."

The white wedding gown has a long history, though not one quite as ancient as might be suggested by the popularity, in recent years, of medieval-style gowns with drooping bell-shaped sleeves, which owe more to the *Lord of the Rings* movies than they do to historical precedent. White was worn by young women as a marker of maidenhood as early as the sixteenth century, but was not always the preferred choice for brides—the poorer of whom, for centuries, would most likely be married in whatever they owned that was newest and cleanest, while the wealthy opted for rich brocades and silks. By the 1830s and 1840s, white had become a coveted choice for brides of higher social position: It signified not just purity but wealth, since white was an expensive color to keep clean. Its status as the desideratum of bridal style was decisively established by the example of Queen Victoria, who, as a nineteen-year-old bride in 1840, wore a white gown with a deep neckline, tightly corseted waist, and sleeves as puffed as a freshly baked popover; but it remained an option reserved for the affluent. A bridal portrait taken toward the end of the nineteenth century might show a woman dressed in a dark gown that has been accented for the occasion with a white lace collar—a modest sartorial accoutrement for a massive personal transformation.

By the 1920s and 1930s, the long, white silk gown had been established as the fashion among those who could afford it, and a burgeoning wedding-dress industry was emerging. America's entry into the Second World War presented the bridal industry with obstacles: Many women were inclined, for the sake of expediency, to marry in something other than a new tailor-made outfit before their grooms were shipped off to war; and when rationing of silk for parachutes was introduced, a trade group called the Bridal and Brides-maids Apparel Association lobbied Congress for an exemption, arguing that they should have access to fabric "for morale purposes." (The lobbying efforts were successful: Said the president of the association some years later, "We told them, 'American boys are going off to war and what are they fighting for except the privilege of getting married in a traditional way?'")

It was not until after the Second World War that marrying in white became the widespread standard, thanks to the availability of mass-produced gowns from synthetic fibers; and while the countercultural movement of the late sixties and the inexorable rise of the institution of divorce were occasions for anxiety among members of the bridal industry, whose gloomier number feared that the traditional American wedding might be going the way of the traditional American nuclear family, such fears proved to be ill founded. (In 1965 the Bridal and Bridesmaids Apparel Association commissioned a survey which discovered, helpfully enough for its purposes, that a bride who wore a long formal gown had twice as much chance of staying married as one who opted for a short dress.) For those members of the avant-garde who did reject the trappings of a conventional wedding, the bridal industry was swift to provide unconventional trappings: In the early seventies, one New York department store opened a salon called The Barefoot Bride, and a window display at Bergdorf Goodman of the same era featured a rough-spun Indian wedding gown, available inside for five hundred dollars. At the outset of the 1980s, the wedding of Prince Charles and Princess Diana—instantly mythologized as a fairy tale come to life—had an immeasurably salutary effect upon the wedding-dress business, with Diana's ball gown spawning countless imitations and members of the wedding industry speaking to the media, with a sigh of relief, about a "return to tradition."

By the end of the twentieth century, the gown that 150 years earlier had been a marker of affluence and social status, had become close to obligatory for all brides, regardless of income or class. Yet unlike other consumer items and services that have moved from being the preserve of the few to the province of the many—television sets, airline travel—the bridal gown has not lost its aura of luxury. In part, this is because even a less expensive wedding dress is still a very expensive item: The respondents to the 2006 Condé Nast Wedding Study paid an average of $1,025 for their dresses. But the aura of luxury does not derive simply from the gown's cost. It is inherent in the means of the gown's production. After experiencing "the 'Oh, Mommy' moment" when she tries on the gown that for her is the One, the bride will ultimately be provided with a gown which, she will be told, has been specially made for her and her alone.

Bridal gowns are not sold in the same way as televisions or airline tickets are, not in independent bridal stores at least. Brides such as the music teacher at the Bridal Mall try on a store sample before an order is placed with the manufacturer for a new dress, which will arrive months later to be altered to fit by an in-house seamstress. It is a central tenet of the independent bridal business that a client, at least a well-behaved one, will relish this drawn-out process rather than feel frustrated by it: that the bride who has probably never worn any garment requiring more alteration than the turning up of a hem, and most of whose clothes cling to her courtesy of Lycra rather than the skill of a seamstress, will appreciate service over speed. Barbara Barrett, for example, offers preceremony visitation for gowns she holds in storage, so that her clients have the opportunity to show the chosen garment to select friends and family, and on weekends, the Bridal Mall can resemble a petting zoo, filled with women cooing over the tulle.

In spite of the industry rhetoric of their uniqueness, most bridal gowns are not actually made to measure, except in the cases of extremely high-end, one-of-a-kind gowns. Rather they are mass produced according to the orders placed with overseas factories, before being shipped to the stores for alteration. The music teacher's gown will not come off the factory floor ready for her to step into, but will merely be a closer approximation to her size than the sample she tried on in the first place. It will, however, be completely new, and the virgin quality of the gown is something that is stressed by bridal-store owners to their customers as part of the specialness of the experience. It might be said that the unsullied gown does not represent the purity of the bride, as white wedding gowns of old did, but substitutes for it, now that the bride's purity is by no means assured or in many cases expected.

Because each bride's gown is virgin, and altered to fit her and only her, it plays into her fantasies of uniqueness—even if its origin on the production line of a Chinese factory floor is decidedly lacking in romance, and even if the wearing of the gown actually inducts her into the regulations of a conforming mass. She is both a singular incarnation and Everybride: her best self and the culture's cynosure.

At the Bridal Mall, as at the three thousand other independent bridal retailers around the country, there is little room for sentimentality about wedding dresses, or about the brides who wear them. The wedding dress retail business is a very competitive one, since there is a limited pool of brides whose custom may be gained. While Bridezilla culture may be on the ascendant, actual rates of marriage are on the decline: 7.6 per thousand of the population in 2004, compared with a rate of 10.5 twenty years earlier. As Gary Wright, the head of an industry association called the National Bridal Service, told me, the wedding-gown business is "the purest example of an inelastic market. No one has yet found a way to increase the demand. No one ever says, 'This is a great time to get married—the bridal store is having a sale.'"

As a consequence, bridal-store owners, at least those who want their businesses to flourish, are required to foster Bridezilla culture—even as they understandably recoil from their most demanding and impossible-to-please customers. (When I visited Barbara Barrett in Niantic she told me, wearily, that she had been sued in small-claims court by one bride who contended that the fit of her dress had restricted her ability to dance at her wedding reception twelve months earlier, a trauma that had persisted throughout her first year of marriage.) The selling of the dress is only part of what is required. It is a rule of thumb among bridal retailers that whatever a bride has spent on her dress she should be persuaded to spend again on a veil, a tiara, jewelry, shoes, undergarments, and other fripperies; and one article from *Vows* magazine, the trade publication for the wedding-dress retail industry, explains how to do just that, reminding its readers that "Just when the bride thinks she'll have to spend no more, it's your job to remind her that her bridal image looks incomplete."

"You celebrate the fact that you've helped her finally commit to one magical gown, a pair of delicate pumps, an angelic veil and a sparkling tiara that solidifies her brideliness," the article reported. "[But] forfeit the plastic, hang onto that celebratory enthusiasm, and stay focused just a bit longer. It's time to sell some jewelry." It's also, apparently, time to sell long wedding gloves, in spite of brides' dislike of them: "The most common objection keeping customers from warming up to this accessory is convenience. Brides don't want the hassle of wearing something they will remove during the ceremony," the *Vows* author noted. Purses are an even more difficult sale. "The most common reason brides don't buy a purse is because they don't want to carry it around on their wedding day . . . they don't want to be encumbered," the magazine reported. "Admittedly this is a difficult objection to combat, but you still need to try." While every bride who comes to a bridal store will probably end up buying a white gown of some kind, whether or not she purchases the full complement of bridal accessories depends in part upon the skill of the salesperson attending her; and the profits of the store depend, in turn, upon that. At the Bridal Mall, Barbara Barrett showed me a silver-plated crystal tiara that retailed for about $250, saying as she did so, "This is the piece that pays the bills."

Declining marriage rates are not the independent retailers' only problem. Beginning in the 1990s they have been faced with a formidable competitor: David's Bridal, the only nationwide chain of bridal stores, which has brought the contemporary principles of mass marketing to what had hitherto been exclusively a specialty business. David's Bridal has more than 250 stores nationwide, and now dresses one in four of all American brides. Among independent bridal retailers, the company is regarded much as is Barnes & Noble by independent booksellers: a giant interloper who has unilaterally changed the rules of the game. It sells dresses straight off the rack, so that a bride who is getting married one afternoon can waltz into David's Bridal, try on a gown in a size that actually fits her, and be fully accoutred that morning. (Of course, if she really wants it to fit well, she'll probably need alterations, but at least she won't have to wait months for the dress to be delivered before the house seamstress can get her hands on it.) While the company's marketing does not present a David's gown as anything so déclassé as a budget option, it does present it as an affordable one; and it offers the bride who is accustomed to shopping at Old Navy or Banana Republic the reassurance of a purchase made from a brand with which she is familiar, if only because she has seen the David's logo—with a heart for an apostrophe—at the mall or on a highway sign before she has ever had reason to consult a bridal magazine.

These are all attributes of the consumer experience that the independent retailers of wedding gowns maintain are deleterious, to the bride's experience as well as to their own bottom line. "The bridal industry has always provided for this one time in a woman's life when she plans a huge social event, and the bridal salons have treated them like princesses," says Barbara Barrett. "We hate to turn bridal shopping into a Wal-Mart or Kmart experience." Barrett, who opened the Bridal Mall in 1993, before David's Bridal was a significant player in the wedding-dress marketplace, told me she will not allow a woman carrying a David's Bridal garment bag to cross her threshold, even if it means losing a lucrative veil-and-tiara sale. "We have three David's Bridal stores in Connecticut and one in Rhode Island, and I'm told that each of those stores expects to sell three thousand dresses a year," Barrett said with a grimace. "In the entire state of Connecticut there are only twelve thousand brides a year, so David's wants three-quarters of the market. At my store, we're keeping our heads above water because a lot of other smaller shops have already closed. But if all you did was keep your name in the Yellow Pages, you are toast."

Conshohocken, Pennsylvania, where David's Bridal is based, is one of those nineteenth-century towns where the remnants of industrial infrastructure provide a pleasant setting for industries whose profits depend less than those of earlier times on the deployment of working-class muscle and the burning of fossil fuels. There is a railway track, now disused. There is a canal, now leafy and unhurried. A former foundry houses David's Bridal's headquarters, which is equipped with a fancy cafeteria, a staff gymnasium, and cubicles and conference rooms whose calm hum is indistinguishable from that of a prosperous insurance office.

My guide was Gary Schwartz, then the company's senior vice president for marketing, who was handsome—he could have been a model for After Hours, the tuxedo-rental company that is part of the David's Bridal operation—and had a deep and resonant voice. Schwartz met me in the airy lobby of the David's building, where there were comfortable armchairs artfully placed in casual groupings, and took me out to the parking lot, where we climbed into his Porsche and took off for the Metroplex shopping center in nearby Plymouth Meeting to visit a David's store.

"We are trying to use this store as a concept tester, from our ability to monitor it from a numbers and visual standpoint," Schwartz explained as we drove along. Schwartz had the ability to conduct a friendly conversation entirely in language that might have been lifted from an annual report. "We can make or break that wedding day, and we have got to be sensitive, just from a life's-experience point of view."

The original David's Bridal, which was opened in the 1950s by one David Reisberg, was a single store in Fort Lauderdale, Florida. In the early seventies Reisberg sold his store to a young entrepreneur named Phil Youtie, who decided to keep the established name. Youtie, the son of an amusement park operator from Philadelphia, went on to buy up existing bridal stores all over Florida, in Boca Raton and in Coral Gables, and turned them into David's stores as well.

Like all bridal stores at the time, David's Bridal stocked only sample gowns in a standard size. Youtie, however, began to consider that different models might be applied. By the 1980s outlet malls at which discontinued merchandise was sold at discounted prices had emerged in the field of ready-to-wear; and in 1991, inspired by this example, Youtie and a childhood friend named Steve Erlbaum opened a bare-bones bridal warehouse operation on I-95 in Hallandale, Florida. David's Bridal Wearhouse, as it was then known, had no carpets, no dressing rooms, and sold manufacturers' overstocks of dresses that were half the price they would have been in salons.

"The first year, we made an enormous profit, because we had an unheard-of markup," Youtie told me when I called him in Florida, where he is now retired. "We did no alterations, and if anyone needed a bobby pin, we would charge them for it." When manufacturers realized that David's was undercutting their business they became less willing to offload their unsold dresses, so Youtie took his trade overseas and began working directly with manufacturers of gowns in Taiwan to make David's brand-name dresses. Over the subsequent years more branches of David's opened, gradually becoming less like warehouses and more like conventional stores, with dressing rooms and carpets. In 1999, Youtie and Erlbaum took the company public for more than $100 million; and in 2000, the May Department Stores Company, which also owned Famous-Barr, Filene's, and Strawbridge's, bought David's for $436 million. (In 2005, the May company was itself taken over by Federated Department Stores, Inc., which owns Macy's and Bloomingdale's. In 2006, Federated sold David's Bridal to a private equity firm, Leonard Green & Partners, for $750 million.)

The Metroplex shopping center, to which Gary Schwartz took me, is home to big-box stores like Target, Old Navy, and Bed, Bath & Beyond, set in sprawling acres of parking lot upon which huge, emptied shopping carts have been abandoned, like chariots vanquished in battle. When we entered David's Bridal, which looked much like every other David's store around the country, with pale peach and green decor so bland it seems as if the store designer has given the instruction to make it look like Ann Taylor, only less edgy. "Our Love Is Here to Stay" was playing tinnily over the audio system. On the clothing racks, hundreds of dresses jostled one another for space like New York City subway riders at rush hour.

The average store, Schwartz explained, has in stock one thousand to twelve hundred bridal gowns in a range of sizes and styles, most of them available for purchase off the rack. On a weekday a customer can just walk into a store to shop for a dress, but on Saturdays and Sundays, when the stores are at their busiest, an appointment is advised. Even with an appointment, Schwartz warned, the place could be a bit of a madhouse. "There are days when we can deliver what the perception of an appointment is, and days when it's difficult," he admitted. There were 135 different styles to choose from in the formal section, where the dresses were bead-encrusted or decked in lace with skirts so voluminous they could suffice for a parachute jump. "These are more traditional," Schwartz said, and when I asked what David's meant by "traditional," he said, "It could be anything, from a long-sleeved wedding dress onward. It depends what your *idea* of that tradition is." In the informal section the gowns were more like something an aspiring starlet would wear on a movie premiere's red carpet, in the hope that the gown's unstructured neckline might display a glimpse of cleavage at a photo-graphically strategic moment. "That's for when you are flying to Jamaica and you don't want to walk on the beach in twelve hundred dollars' worth of bead-ing," Schwartz explained. Toward the rear of the store was the Oleg Cassini Collection—a higher-priced line designed by the sometime couturier for Jacqueline Kennedy. The Cassini gowns, Schwartz explained, had superior boning to David's regular gowns and more expensive fabrication. He rum-maged around inside one—it had stiff, embroidery-covered skirts and was priced at $750—and found a fabrication label that read 100% POLYESTER. Schwartz quickly stuffed the label back in the dress. "There are polyester fabrics now that are more expensive than silk," he said.

The size of the David's operation, and the fact that David's stores are dis-tributed all over the country, means that the company's database of customer information reveals trends and tastes among brides and differences in de-mographics, and permits David's to respond. "Mormons require certain things to be covered up in the ceremony, but they want less coverage in the reception, so there we have tried to do things with detachables," Schwartz said. Because David's sells bridesmaids' dresses and offers a tuxedo-rental service, the company is able to track shopping patterns to determine when a bride typically shops for different wedding components. With that informa-tion, David's can send its new brides reminders of its product offerings long after the initial purchase of the dress, thus continuing to engage with the customer over a period of months. "The first product the bride buys is the dress, typically seven months ahead of the wedding," Schwartz said. "Tuxedos generally get bought five to six months after the wedding gown; bridesmaids' dresses, three to four months. So we become the lead generator for all the processes after."

We were there on a Friday, and only a few customers were making their way around the aisles or changing in the fitting area at the rear of the store, where there was a long bank of mirrors. One woman who looked to be in her mid-thirties was trying on a strapless gown with a lace-up bodice, while nearby a little girl with blond curls, evidently the bride's daughter, was staring covetously at a rack of diminutive dresses with full tulle skirts. "There's a typical second wedding," said Schwartz. "Much less formal gown."

I watched as the bride maneuvered in front of the mirrors in her dress, which, while not exactly formal—it looked like something a Victorian lady might have put on underneath her actual wedding gown—was nonetheless unlike any gown this woman was likely to have worn before (apart from whatever she wore at her first wedding). She looked at herself in the mirror, sizing up the vision before her, waiting and hoping for her "'Oh, Mommy' moment," even though she was already a mommy herself. For the bride shopping at David's—no less than for the bride shopping at the Bridal Mall—the store's sophisticated marketing methods meant little; and while the consumer convenience of trying on a dress in her own size and being able to buy it off the rack might be different, the underlying emotional experience was not. To her, the dress was not a lead generator but a dream generator.

The dress that prompted the music teacher's "'Oh, Mommy' moment" at the Bridal Mall in Connecticut had found its way there after being selected by Barbara Barrett from among hundreds of dresses on display at the National Bridal Market, the nation's biggest trade show for the bridal industry. The

National Bridal Market takes place twice a year in Chicago, at The Merchandise Mart, an enormous art deco complex on the Chicago River; and to visit there is to see wedding dresses not as singular, precious artifacts, as Chip Eichelberger's listeners hoped their customers would, but as bridal-store owners do: as a mass of remarkably similar product, from which winners—the dresses that will take the customer's breath away—must be plucked and losers—the dresses that will end up on the sale rack—skirted.

The aura of exclusivity and luxury that is promoted by bridal stores and in the fashion pages of bridal magazines is nowhere to be found at the Chicago market, which feels like a giant wedding souk, with enough dresses to marry the entire population of South Korea in one enormous Moonie ceremony; tiaras sufficient to restore every deposed monarchy in history; enough shoes in white and gold and glasslike plastic to equip a marching army of Cinderellas; and veils for a thousand and one Scheherazades. When I went to the Chicago market one October, I browsed the aisles, watching as the manufacturers staged miniature fashion shows for the retailers, and trying to distinguish between brands whose names seemed lifted from dusty, half-empty cut-glass perfume bottles: Jovani; Joan Calabrese; Anjolique; Bel Aire; Rivini. After a few hours I was overcome by a condition known among retailers as "white blindness," a reeling, dumbfounded state in which it becomes impossible to distinguish between an Empire-waisted gown with alençon lace appliqués and a bias-cut spaghetti-strap shift with crystal detail, and in the exhausted grip of which I wanted only to lie down and be quietly smothered by the fluffy weight of it all, like Scott of the Antarctic.

The social highlight of the National Bridal Market was an awards ceremony held at the Field Museum of Natural History, with cocktails served in a hall so lofty that it made Sue, the museum's prized forty-two-foot Tyrannosaurus rex skeleton, look like a small house pet provided with a very grand, very spacious, all-marble kennel. The DEBIs—the acronym derives from

Distinctive Elegance in the Bridal Industry—were presented in the museum's plush theater: prizes for bridal gowns and for bridesmaids' gowns, as well as for Outstanding Accessory Resource—in other words, the best shoes designed specifically to be completely concealed under a wedding dress, for which examples of the competing footwear were tap-danced across the stage by a group of beaming chorus girls—and Outstanding Headpiece award, for which a series of models in bridal attire swanned before the footlights and everyone applauded their veils.

David's Bridal's alarming contributions to the bridal marketplace went unmentioned until there was an uncomfortable comic interlude, during which executives from three gown companies—Marty Boikess from Mori Lee; Stanley Goldstein from Rena Koh; and Jerry Smale from Mon Cheri—shuffled out from the wings, dressed in tuxedos and sunglasses and looking slightly self-conscious. The host for the evening, Jasmine Guy, from *A Different World,* said to the trio, "Your mission, should you choose to accept it, is to take out David's!" upon which each of the three delivered a tough-guy line. "David's will sleep with the fishes," said Boikess. "Hasta la vista, baby," added Goldstein. "Go ahead, make my David's," said Smale, with a smirk. Then they all shuffled off stage again, to great applause from the audience. Like the wedding planners at the Business of Brides barbecue who enacted a ritual wedding to mock the customers upon whom they depended and, at the same time, resented, the retailers and the manufacturers in Chicago seemed to be attempting to neuter the threat of David's through a symbolic diminishment. The attempt, like the barbecue skit, was pretty lame, but it was the best they could do in the face of an aggressor that threatened to do to them what history had done to Sue, the Tyrannosaurus rex.

One of the last awards to be given out, for Outstanding Special Occasion Gowns/Eveningwear, went to Montage by Mon Cheri, and was accepted by Steve Lang, the company's president. He had a message about David's, too.

"Someone said earlier that this is a glamorous industry, but it is not as much fun as it used to be," Lang said with an air of practiced sanctimony, like a Sunday school teacher. "I want everyone to take your right hand and put it on your heart and say, 'I am going to become a happier person.' We have to fight a common enemy, not one another. Let's bring back the fun, and let's use that four letter word: *love.*"

That weddings have anything much to do with love is not a fact that is easy to keep in mind amid the commercial bustle of the National Bridal Market. And the promotion of love among the manufacturers and retailers at the market seemed improbable, given that all are competing for the business of a limited number of brides. It is a little hard, at the National Bridal Market, to square the optimistic perspective on the wedding industry presented by Condé Nast's annual wedding studies with what seems to be the reality on the ground, at least in this sector of the wedding industry: that for all the excesses of Bridezilla culture, making a living from selling wedding dresses is hard to do.

Part of the reason for this is that, while high-end designers such as Monique Lhuillier or Vera Wang, whose gowns cost from the mid-four figures up to twenty thousand dollars and beyond, may be thriving, and while the mass-marketing strategy of David's Bridal is doing well, the middle of the market, that occupied by the independent bridal retailers and the manufacturers who supply them, is being squeezed. (Independent retailers typically offer dresses at very similar price points to David's, but without the same profit margins that David's is able to command through economies of scale.) This squeezing of the middle is a tendency apparent in many dimensions of retail, with Americans filling their wardrobes with both designer purchases and dirt-cheap goods from Target or Wal-Mart; and in the bridal business it is happening no less, even though a low-end dress, at four or five hundred dollars, is hardly inexpensive. The mass availability of less costly wedding dresses at David's and at the independent retailers obliged to compete with David's may be a boon to the bride who wants to wear one, but for retailers like Barbara Barrett, and for the manufacturers celebrated at the DEBI awards, diminishing profit margins are unwelcome indeed. They also serve as an encouragement to the bridal retailers to push accessories purchases even harder, so that the bride will compensate for the retailer's lost dress profits by buying, for example, white bridal shoes, which, as the trade magazine *Vows* advises, are "easy cash in the pocket" and "a nice little chunk that adds up." (An advertisement in *Vows* for the Dyeables shoe company reads, "She spent five years finding 'him.' He spent five months choosing the ring. She doesn't need to know it only took you five minutes to order her shoes.")

The wholesale and retail prices of wedding dresses have fallen because their production has moved offshore. Until the 1980s, the majority of dresses worn by ordinary American brides were made domestically, but by the mid-eighties, Taiwanese imports began to appear at the semiannual bridal markets. At first their quality was poor, with glued beading that came unstuck while the models walked on the temporary aisles. The initial reaction of the American manufacturers was contempt: at one market Alfred Angelo, a company that was founded in the 1930s in Philadelphia and has remained a family business ever since, put American flags in their showroom and served apple pie to buyers. But an inexorable transformation was under way. Taiwanese manufacturers could make dresses at a fraction of the price of their American competitors, and they were quick to improve the standards of handiwork. Before long, continuing to make dresses in the United States became, for most bridal manufacturers, economic idiocy, and more and more companies moved their manufacturing offshore—including the patriotic Alfred Angelo, which took its business from Philadelphia to Guatemala. Meanwhile dozens of new companies started up whose manufacturing operations were based in Taiwan and, increasingly, in China proper, where factories filled with migrant workers sprung up to produce hundreds of thousands of dresses, around the clock, at a rock-bottom labor cost.

The American bridal business, once dominated by white ethnics, has become increasingly populated by Asian American entrepreneurs; and one evening in the bar of the Holiday Inn, where exhibitors and buyers at the Chicago market gather at the end of the day to trade gossip and relax, I was introduced to one of them: Nick Yeh, the president of a company called Impression Bridal. Yeh was dressed as if for a night on the town in South Beach or SoHo rather than for an evening in a dowdy hotel bar: in a Versace suit with a knee-length jacket, a thin leather tie, and tinted eyeglasses, with his straight black hair gelled into an improbable pompadour.

Yeh has a reputation as one of the smartest of the new bridal entrepreneurs—as adept at operating on the floor of the Merchandise Mart in Chicago as at doing business in China, in the great wedding-dress workshops of the East. Yeh was born in Vietnam to Chinese parents and went into the wedding business in the early nineties. The energy of the industry in China is incredible, he told me. "If you go to China, you don't even feel that it is Communist," he said. "To me, it is similar to the U.S. The buildings are different, and the culture is different, but it is as free a culture as the U.S." He said he went four times a year to the factory that makes his dresses, which was in the city of Xiamen. "We have six hundred people working there," he said. "They live there, in the factory living quarters. There's a dining room for three or four hundred people. It's almost like a village."

I asked if next time he went he would take me along.

"Sure," he said.

Xiamen has the aspect of a perpetual construction site, with shimmering metallic office towers and luxury apartment blocks set among thickets of cranes and construction machinery, the shrubs and trees planted in the roadway medians dusty from the relentless demolition. Known in the past to foreigners as Amoy, the city has a long history as an important port, though its economic development was abruptly curtailed when the Communists came to power in 1949 and its coastal position, not far from Taiwan, suddenly became a political liability rather than an asset. In the 1980s a Special Economic Zone was established in Xiamen, in which economic expansion and foreign investment was encouraged, and since then, the city has boomed. The population has grown from 930,000 in 1980 to more than 1.5 million in 2005, and the city's gross domestic product, which in 1980 was 0.64 billion yuan—about $80 million—had, by 2005, reached 102.96 billion yuan, the equivalent of almost $13 billion.

For all its growth the city still feels spacious and uncrowded, as if it were nowhere near its full capacity and were still just ramping up for the future. There are pleasant parks for the amusement of the residents, as well as miles of attractive coastline, although the building of a highway, snaking on concrete stilts along a section of the beachfront, has undermined the scenic attractions somewhat. Shopping malls are thronged with Chinese consumers: electronics stores selling air conditioners and mobile phones of designs not yet available in the United States, and clothing boutiques—including one called "Life in US"—selling cheap, fashionable styles. Xiamen has two Wal-Mart stores that sell, in addition to the kind of consumer goods familiar in the U.S. stores, vacuum-packed squid and quilted satin pajamas and bottles of Great Wall cabernet sauvignon, and at the doors employees stand and bellow greetings to customers, according to the company's international standards of hospitality.

On my first morning in Xiamen, I went with Yeh to the Top Fashion factory, where Yeh's dresses were being made. We were with two of Yeh's colleagues: Ron Calk, an energetic young salesman covering the southern United States, whom it was easier to imagine crossing the country as a bass player in an alternative band than peddling dresses to stores in Oklahoma and Baton Rouge; and Ruben Cruz, who teaches formal-wear design at the Fashion Institute of Technology in New York City and designs gowns for Impression Bridal. Top Fashion, which is owned by a Taiwanese businessman named Eric Wang, was on the industrial outskirts of the city. (Taiwan is only about 190 miles from Xiamen as the crow flies, and ferry boats take eager Chinese tourists out into the straits to snap photographs of the Taiwanese island Quemoy's undistinguished coastline. The Taiwanese residents of Xiamen are obliged, owing to their homeland's fraught sovereignty dispute with China, to take a more circuitous route home, via Macao or Hong Kong.) On the way out of town we passed some familiar brand names—Dell and TDK—among the light-industrial factories that edged the highway. Amid the development were occasional plots of land that had not yet been built upon: patches of vivid green rice paddies tended by laborers in conical hats, buckets slung on poles balanced on their shoulders, looking as if they were posing for a calendar photograph of timeless rural China.

It is from rural China—which is not timeless, as it turns out, but increasingly outpaced by comparison with the new industrial centers, and lacking the economic support once provided by the central government—that come most of the employees at Top Fashion, whose handiwork I was shortly to witness. There are at least three wedding-dress factories besides Top Fashion in Xiamen, also owned by Taiwanese businessmen; but that is nothing compared with the city of Chaozhou, which is known as the world capital of wedding-dress production. Chaozhou is in Guangdong Province, near Hong Kong, and is home to more than 550 apparel factories, including the enormous Famory factory, which was established by the state in the 1940s, employs 2,600 workers, and produces, in addition to half a million evening dresses, 150,000 wedding dresses a year, the vast majority of which are destined for the international market. Almost all the mass-market dresses sold in the United States—including those sold at David's Bridal and at the Bridal Mall in Connecticut—start out in factories like these.

As we drove along, Nick Yeh revisited some of the themes I had heard discussed in Chicago. "The bridal stores say they don't want to sell the same dresses as David's, they want to be a *salon*," he said. "Well, wake up—they took twenty-five percent of your business." (One response to the threat presented by David's Bridal has been that of the Emme Bridal company, which is run by Nick Yeh's brother, Michael Yeh, and which launched a line of David's look-alike dresses to be sold in independent stores cheekily called DaVinci Bridal.) Yeh liked to think of himself as a business-minded philistine: He never read books, he told me, and scorned any interest in culture beyond the culture of making money. His all-business brusqueness masked a likeable generosity, though, and he had a sense of humor and a winning amplitude of appetite. While we were in Xiamen, I asked Yeh whether he spoke any languages other than Chinese and English. "I speak some Italian," he said. *"Gucci, Versace."*

The factory looked from the outside rather like a suburban middle school. Inside high gates, past the gatehouse, there was a complex of four-story buildings surrounded by ornamental beds of shrubbery. A shaded area was planted with trees and climbing vines and provided with benches, and a single basketball hoop was set above a driveway. Eric Wang, who spoke English and some Spanish—he also makes dresses for Pronovias, a company based in Madrid—had a bright, jocular manner, as if he were perpetually trying out for a part in a sitcom. He showed me around the factory, starting on the ground floor, where the dress fabric arrives in twenty-foot bales of artificial silk from South Korea or India, where it is made. The bales are examined under bright light for flaws before being hefted into the cutting room and chopped into skirt and bodice panels. The cutters are all men, most of them, their female supervisor explained, married to female Top Fashion workers, who dominate the workforce of 520. Next to the cutting room was the enormous sewing department, with seventy workstations packed into narrow rows. Half of the seamstresses were bent over their machines making bodices, while the other half were stitching skirt panels together. Everyone was wearing a jacket embroidered with the Top Fashion logo, as uniform as a Mao suit.

"That's one of Nick's dresses," Wang said, pointing to an indeterminate pool of white fabric. "We make about a hundred thousand dresses a year, half of them for the U.S. market. Nick's our best customer."

Wang explained that the workers were paid by the piece: For each finished skirt, of which it is possible for an accomplished seamstress to produce perhaps fifteen per day, she earned about forty cents. The average monthly wage at Top Fashion, according to Wang, was about U.S. $150 per month. This is not a bad sum as Chinese factory wages go, although labor costs account for only a fraction of the dress's ultimate retail price, which is likely to be the equivalent of more than four months' wages.

The workday began at eight; there was a ninety-minute break for lunch and a nap at noon, and then work began again, continuing until five-thirty. Overtime, should the production load demand it, often had the workers at their stations until nine or ten at night. There was usually a six-day workweek, though, when Yeh and I were visiting, the factory was on a seven-day schedule, since the Chinese New Year was approaching and there were orders to fill before the holiday. As a weekend perk, workers were allowed on Saturdays to listen to the radio on the shop floor, although the rest of the time there was no sound but the whirring of sewing machines. I was struck by the intensity of the workers—the absence of even the briefest conversation between neighbors. "They don't have time to talk to each other," Wang said. "They don't make money that way."

Upstairs was another enormous room full of workers in Top Fashion jackets. Dull green drapes had been drawn across all the windows to keep out the heat of the sun. (Temperatures in Xiamen can go above one hundred in the summer, and its winters are mild; the factory has air-conditioning vents set into the ceiling to prevent even the most tireless worker from dripping sweat onto a gown.) Here, Wang explained, was where the detail and trimming was added to the dress. The major beading work was done off the premises, but twenty women were assigned to the task of stitching on by hand any beads that had been missed, and they sat, bent around a large table, sewing white on white.

On the other side of the room was the lace-application department, where an industrious production line was in place turning out gowns for hundreds of potential Cinderellas to wear to the ball. The first woman expertly pinned lengths and patches of lace to a skirt, which was then passed on to her colleague at a sewing machine. The sewing-machine operator slid the fabric into place under her needle, stepped on the power, and then stitched around the complex lace patterns, rapidly turning her hands left and right as if she were at the wheel of a Formula One race car. The finished piece was handed off to a third woman, who sat with a plastic bucket at her feet into which she tossed the pins which she swiftly pulled from the fabric, like a farmer's wife plucking a hen. "Her salary is based on the weight of the pins," Wang said. "Otherwise they would let them drop everywhere. For a kilo, she's paid two U.S. dollars."

At noon, a bell rang for lunch, and the workers trooped out of the factory and along a pathway to an enormous, hangarlike dining hall that was equipped with trestle tables and plastic stools, where they lined up to receive a lunch of rice, meat, and vegetables served in a divided metal tray, like a TV dinner. The Impression Bridal team didn't go to the dining hall, but to the Wangs' large family house, which sat next door to the main factory building. Several other Chinese men arrived for lunch—garment-business colleagues—and a lazy Susan was set in the middle of the table, piled with dishes. Yeh helped himself from a plate of what he said were pigs' ears, snack-sized morsels of what looked like very salty, chewy meat. Shot glasses were brought out, as was a bottle of 53-proof alcohol, and the visiting Chinese businessmen—one of whom, I later discovered when he brought out his merchandise for our inspection, manufactured gel-filled, flesh-colored fake breasts of the sort that can be slipped into a bra for extra volume—started playing a drinking game.

After lunch Yeh and the rest of the team went to the design department, on the third floor of the factory, to look over the new samples that Wang had produced. We left our shoes outside the door of the showroom, not out of any observance of ancient custom but because outdoor footwear is banned in proximity to the merchandise for fear of soiling the fabric. Inside, rows of dresses hung on racks, and three tailors' dummies stood at attention. A conference table was spread with papers: design drawings that Ruben Cruz had faxed over, as well as pages of advertisements ripped from bridal magazines. "Nick gives me a picture, and then we have to guess what the back and the hemline look like," said Wang. "He's a troublemaker."

Three dresses at a time were pulled off the racks and hoisted onto the dummies for Yeh, Cruz, and Ron Calk to look at. A princess-cut gown embroidered with colored flowers, and an off-white gown with spaghetti straps and a coffee-colored sash, both proven crowd-pleasers, were given the nod for production. A third gown with scallop-edged tiers descending from its bodice all the way down its skirt to the floor was quickly dismissed. "We must have been drunk when we did that one," said Yeh.

In some cases the front and back of the dress were weirdly mismatched— a lace trim on the waist ended abruptly as it rounded the rib cage; the rear panels of a skirt were made from an entirely different fabric than were those at the front—as if the patterns had been put together by someone who had not conceived of the dress actually being seen in three dimensions. "You can't have lace like this—it has to go all the way around," Cruz said, looking at one peculiar hybrid gown.

"You want to pay the extra lace charge?" asked Wang.

"You want to get the orders?" said Cruz.

A pale, salmon-colored dress covered with a floral pattern was brought out. Cruz took a closer look. "This is embroidery," he said. "It should be alençon lace. Lace is what people are buying."

There was anxious muttering among the Chinese design team, for whom Cruz's words were translated by Jennifer Wang, Eric Wang's daughter. Someone fetched a roll of lace fabric, which Cruz laid down on top of the satin to show what he had envisaged. There was more muttering from one of the Chinese design team.

"What is she saying?" Cruz asked Jennifer Wang.

Jennifer looked embarrassed. "She's saying it's ugly," she said.

The next dress was another scalloped gown, with a ruched frill around the neckline. It looked like the kind of dress that would head straight for the remaindered rack and might eventually be bought as a bride-of-Frankenstein Halloween costume.

"Oh my God, no," said Cruz.

"I think it's kind of cool," said Ron Calk, still red-eyed from lunch.

"Cool doesn't put money in your pocket or my pocket," Yeh said decisively. "What's next?"

The following day, Yeh had to drive to another factory to look at bridesmaids' gowns, and so I went back to Top Fashion alone, where I met Jennifer Wang, who showed me around the workers' living quarters. Most of the workers had come to work in Xiamen from provinces farther north, where jobs were scarcer, and so Top Fashion was not just a workplace but a home. Accommodation was free, though workers were charged about $7.50 per month for their meals.

The women's dormitory was a four-story block just steps away from the Wangs' family home. We opened the door to a workers' room, which, like all the other, identical rooms, was home to eight young women. It was perhaps 120 feet square, most of that space being occupied by four sets of narrow, metal-framed bunk beds. The bed frames had been hung with gauzy sheets, creating bunk-sized zones of privacy. In the corner of the room there was a table set with an electric kettle and packets of tea and instant noodles. The bathroom, just off the sleeping area, was equipped with two squat toilets behind rough, wooden doors, and a long, troughlike basin, caddies with toothbrushes and combs set along its edge.

There was only cold water in the bathroom, Jennifer explained; for hot water, the women would file out of the dormitory building and across the pathway to an enormous shower room adjacent to the dining hall. A huge hot-water tank sat in the middle of the shower room, which was edged with about forty individual stalls behind fabric curtains, like a changing room in a shabby municipal swimming pool. Above the dining hall was a large, barren recreation room. Judging from the facilities provided—a single TV, which was set into the wall, two pool tables, and several racks of drying clothes—the chief recreation was laundry.

Inside the factory, Jennifer took me to the quality-control department—the last chance for a misaligned seam to be caught, or a forgotten bead to be sewn on, before the dresses were turned inside out and baled up like plump pillowcases, then packed into boxes for shipping to the United States. One of the workers, a stocky woman less than five feet tall, with round, ruddy cheeks, was halfway through checking a batch of plus-size gowns. As we approached, she was hefting a size-30 gown onto an enormous off-white tailor's dummy. She was wearing a black sweater and a plaid tunic, and over her sweater she wore a pair of pull-on sleeves made from a pale, silky fabric to protect the dress as she handled it. Her arms, spilling over with crinoline and tulle, could barely encircle the dummy's waist, and her head reached only as high as the top of the gown's bodice. It was as if, in a magical reversal of roles, a tiny child's doll had come to life and was now able to dress and undress her rigid, massive mistress.

Her name was Tan Lingli, she said as Wang translated, and she had worked at Top Fashion for eleven years, arriving in Xiamen from her home in a much poorer city in Sichuan Province after a friend suggested that she might find work at the factory. She was married, although she only saw her husband, who lived nearby, once a week: The hours and the overtime made it easier for her to live in the dormitories. The hardest part about the job, she said with downcast eyes, was seeing her husband and her child so little. Her ten-year-old-son—the one child she was permitted to have in accordance with the government's population-control policy—lived with his grandparents in Sichuan, and she got to see him just once a year. She hoped that she might one day be able to send him to college with her earnings, which were two and a half yuan—about thirty cents—an hour.

The dress she was checking had a long train, elaborately sequined and embroidered, and as she and a coworker scanned it for flaws the coworker whispered something to Tan Lingli, who giggled. Wang said to me, "They have a question for you. They want to ask you if there are many fat girls in the United States. She can't imagine how big they are. She thinks that they must have huge beds. They must have everything in a big size."

For the American bride the wearing of a wedding gown presents an opportunity for the bridal fantasy of self-invention, in which a wedding is an opportunity to crystallize her hopes and desires for the life to follow. And Tan Lingli and her coworkers at Top Fashion were inventing themselves as well. They were taking their place in the transformation of China into the world's factory, and, as a consequence, into a consumer culture to rival that of the United States.

There is change afoot, too, in the customs of Chinese weddings them-selves, as I discovered when, after leaving Xiamen, I went to Beijing and I met a man named Shi Kangning, a former high school history teacher who runs one of the best-known and busiest wedding bureaus in the city. The bu-reau, which at the height of wedding season services forty-five weddings per week, provides masters of ceremonies to host the elaborate banquets that are the central celebration in a Chinese wedding. It also offers a photo studio in which the couple can pose for an extensive set of portraits that are shot prior to the ceremony and displayed for guests to see. (Among poorer Chinese cit-izens, like those who work at Top Fashion, it's not unusual to have such pic-tures taken in lieu of actually having a costly banquet.) The studio provides the attire for the portraits: not just traditional Chinese wedding garb, but also Western-style gowns. These are not quite the kind of thing that appears on the cover of *Brides* magazine—no simple elegance—but are covered with gold brocade, like the outfits of European royals in the decades immediately preceding bloody, popular revolts. "More and more, people who are not Christian are getting married in a church," Shi explained through a transla-tor, saying that Chinese weddings, with their endless banquets and their practical jokes at the expense of the bride and groom, are fun for the guests, but that the young people don't really enjoy them. Much more appealing, he said, was the Western-style romantic intimacy that Chinese couples see rep-resented in Hollywood movies.

I had come to China to witness firsthand how the accoutrements of the dreams of American brides were actually manufactured—to see and speak to the workers who produced the gowns that would later be sold with an enticing label reading HAND-BEADED, rich with connotations of exclusivity. There, I discovered that the mythology of the dress was spun out of artificial silk that came in twenty-foot bales; and that the music teacher's gown that would make the groom forget to breathe had earned the seamstress who

sewed its skirts forty cents; and I had seen how one person's luxury is produced by another's labor. But I had also seen, at Shi Kangning's office, the
beginning of something different: that just as Chinese workers were producing dresses to fulfill the fantasies of American brides, America, in its turn,
was producing fantasies for the new brides of the new China.

Five

"Your New $100 Billion Customer"

Colin Cowie, the best-known wedding professional in the country, was seated behind a large desk in his apartment, talking on the phone with a titanium PowerBook open in front of him and a huge window giving onto a view of downtown Manhattan's roofs and water towers behind. He was slim, with dark hair cut fashionably short, very white teeth, long-lashed eyes, and buffed, smoothed skin. He wore foundation, blush, and eyeliner.

"Please excuse the makeup," he said, batting his lengthened eyelashes as he wound up his phone call. "I've just finished a segment for CBS."

Cowie, who started his career twenty-odd years ago as a party planner in South Africa, has wrought from the business of weddings contemporary marketing's utmost achievement: the fashioning of a successful personal brand. He appears on *The Early Show* on CBS, dispensing lifestyle advice—

that morning he had advised viewers on how to throw an all-American TV-watching party by ordering out for pizza, creating a Caesar salad with store-bought dressing, and making a red, white, and blue cocktail from what sounded like a lethal mixture of cranberry juice, vodka, and curaçao—and is also a one of Oprah Winfrey's regulars. Cowie established a reputation in the 1990s as a planner of high-end weddings and parties—he claims that there is no such thing as a Colin Cowie signature style, but from the evidence of his coffee-table book, *Colin Cowie Weddings*, he does appear to favor swamping tents, tables, and vestibules in layers of diaphanous white fabric, as if he were Christo bedecking the Reichstag—but he now does only four or five weddings a year, for very rich or very famous clients.

For me, getting to see Cowie had proved next to impossible. For months I would schedule a meeting only to receive an e-mail with an apology a few days before the appointed date: Colin had to be in Los Angeles unexpectedly (to work on Oprah's Million Dollar Wedding Giveaway) or had been summoned by the royal family of Qatar (for the marriage of the Crown Prince Tamim bin Hamad bin Khalifa Al-Thani: a party for the bride in the palace gardens featured dance floors decorated with cages of exotic birds, fire pits, and a forty-five-piece orchestra from Iraq playing on a stage that was draped and lit so that the musicians, all men, could not see any of the three thousand guests, all women). After the third or fourth time this happened, I began to think that the only way I was ever going to get to see Cowie was if I somehow acquired a billionaire fiancé and a hankering to stage a preposterously extravagant wedding—in a palace on the Saharan sands with my guests sitting on a thousand custom-made silk cushions and my attendants arriving at the ceremony on gold-bedecked camels, or in a Scandinavian castle at midsummer where we would feast on reindeer carpaccio and dance beneath the Northern Lights.

When I did finally meet with Cowie it was shortly after the launch of the latest expansion of his brand: He had been hired by JCPenney in an ambitious bid to revamp the company's bridal registry business. "Everyone has realized that the bride is their potential market," Cowie said by way of explaining his new role for the department store chain, which included devising a sexy black-and-white advertisement campaign that had just appeared in the bridal magazines. It depicted a luxurious beachside wedding in Mexico with Tara Reid, the actress and notorious party girl, playing the bride, and Danny Fuller, the surfing champion, as the groom. (A grinning Cowie appeared in the pictures, too, one of a bunch of good-looking white-linen-clad guests.) "It is very simple," Cowie said. "Eighty-five percent of brides who register with your brand will remain loyal to your brand for the next fifty years." The bride, Cowie told me, "is a marketers' target. She is a slam dunk."

"YOU MARRY A STORE, TOO," read an advertisement for Crate & Barrel's wedding registry that appeared in bridal magazines a few years ago—one that aptly captures the hopes of retail executives when it comes to the bridal market. According to the Condé Nast Wedding Study, American brides registered for $9 billion worth of gifts in 2006—a sum which on its own accounts in part for the high-stakes competition that exists between retailers to woo engaged couples to their stores.

But JCPenney and its rivals are interested in much more than securing the one-time custom of a guest-list full of friends and family, as Cowie suggested. What really concerns the department stores—and their mass-luxury rivals like Crate & Barrel or Pottery Barn—is securing the loyalties of the bride well beyond her wedding day. This was the motivation behind the May Department Stores Company's acquisition in 2000 of the David's Bridal chain: May executives saw an opportunity to intervene in the bride's wedding-planning process well before any other store had a chance to reach her, since research shows that a newly engaged woman starts to think about gowns before she starts thinking about just about anything else. "The May company bought us for two very solid reasons," Robert Huth, David's CEO, told me when I visited the David's Bridal headquarters. "One is our ability to grow and be profitable and be a major contributor in our own right. The other is to give them an entrée to a younger customer who is forming a household and needs many of the products they offer." While the bride sees her gift registry as an exciting opportunity to restock her kitchen with coordinating pots and to equip herself with the kind of table settings appropriate to an adult, married life, the intoxicating prospect offered to the department stores by the wedding registry is that of marrying the bride herself: of winning from her a lifelong commitment as a consumer.

The acquisition of stuff—or, among some ethnic groups, including Italian Americans and Chinese Americans, of cash—on the occasion of a wedding has been a long-standing practice in this country. In *Hands and Hearts: A History of Courtship in America*, published in 1984, Ellen Rothman writes that prior to about 1830 gift-giving was restricted to very close family members, but that by the mid-nineteenth century it had spread to a wider circle of family members and friends, and by the last decades of the nineteenth century couples could expect wedding presents from distant relations, acquaintances, and coworkers. (Rothman writes that basic household items such as sheets or towels were considered inappropriate as gifts, since they implied that a couple or their families could not furnish their own home with staples; far more suitable were luxury objects of varying degrees of uselessness: icecream bowls and silver tongs and cut-glass vases, which would only be brought out on special occasions, if ever.)

Registering for wedding gifts is "one of the most indispensable tools in the entire wedding process," Donna Ferrari, the *Brides* editor, had said at the Wedding March on Madison, and today's brides appear to be in full agreement with that proposition: A survey conducted by *Bridal Guide* magazine of its readers in 2006 found that 96 percent of its respondents planned to register. Not only do brides plan to register; grooms do, too: Ninety percent of respondents said that they would be accompanied by their fiancés when registering, while only a quarter of brides would be accompanied by their mothers.

The involvement of men in registering is a distinct change from practices of the past, and one that speaks to the transformation of at least some tasks that were formerly categorized as a wife's housework into recreation for both the sexes to enjoy. Cooking has become a positively macho pursuit, amply demonstrated by the popularity of Mario Batali and the Iron Chef; and how to choose good barware is the kind of thing much recommended in men's magazines, alongside articles about how to get good abs.

The involvement of men in the registry process may be taken as evidence of a change in gender mores; but it is also a testament to the marketing efforts of companies that have sought to position the creation of a wedding registry as a once-in-a-lifetime opportunity to score highly coveted consumer items, for women and men alike. Target, which established its Club Wedd registry in 1995, was extremely influential in this positioning of registering as fun: It was the first retailer to replace the solicitous registry consultant, bearing clipboard and fine-china counsel, with a scanner gun, thus bringing the spirit of the video-game arcade to the precincts of domesticity. WHAT THEY REALLY WANT is Target's tagline in its Club Wedd advertisements: the wedding registry as the ultimate wish list, as if drawn up for consideration by a very generous Santa.

Whatever the practical contribution wedding gifts make to the lives of their recipients, they have a powerful emotional resonance, too. Receiving gifts after a wedding functions for the bride and groom as decisive, material evidence of the change that has taken place in their relationship—a change that may be otherwise hard to perceive after the drama of the wedding day is over, given the conventions of contemporary premarital relations, in which couples often live together, sleep together, cook together, and engage in many if not all of the intimacies of domestic life. The element of absurdity that accompanies the extensive shopping list that is a bridal registry—the suggestion that a bride and groom who have never before had use for a waffle iron or for a pair of asparagus tongs will suddenly discover they now do—does not imply mere acquisitiveness; it is an expression of the profound hope that married life will, in some way, amount to a different kind of domestic engagement. If the days are long behind us in which a new bride was carried over the threshold of her new home into an intimacy and a responsibility that was entirely unknown to her, then the Williams-Sonoma flatware that arrives, courtesy of UPS, upon the newlyweds' doorstep serves as incontrovertible, material proof that a new chapter of life has indeed been entered upon.

For all its omnipresence, though, the registry, and the etiquette surrounding it, remains fraught. Is it acceptable to indicate on the invitations the store at which one is registered? Appropriate to request that guests ship gifts to a distant address rather than bring them to the wedding? Acceptable to register for sports equipment rather than cookware? (The answers, going by the wedding industry playbook, are: definitely not, though you can indicate preferences on a wedding Web site; certainly, though only if you're asked where the gifts should be sent, since you don't want to be seen assuming you're getting any; and yes, if you want to, though don't be surprised if you are given cut-glass bowls instead.)

One explanation for the discomfort that so often accompanies wedding gift-giving and gift-receipt is that today's couples, who are marrying, on average, in their mid to late twenties, in many cases already have households and the equipment to furnish them; and while they might like a Calphalon sauté pan and a George Foreman grill, they don't exactly need them. Even those who start out with the most, or the means to purchase the most, seem able to find more stuff for their friends to give them: When Donald Trump married Melania Knauss, they registered for gifts that included a Christofle soup ladle and sterling silver pitcher from Tiffany. The institution of the "non-traditional" registry—at Home Depot or at Target or with the Sun Trust Mortgage Company, which permits guests to contribute toward a down payment on a house—means that the range of items which a bride and groom can determine either that they need or that they wish to acquire, has expanded indefinitely, extending well beyond the conceit that the registry enables a couple to stock the kitchen cabinets and the linen closets of a new home. When Ari Fleischer, the former spokesman for George W. Bush, took a public ribbing from *The Washington Post* for the online wish list he and his bride-to-be, Rebecca Davis, assembled at Target—it included a DVD player and some favorite movies, along with household items such as a Michael Graves—designed laundry sorter—what was being mocked was not only the couple's cinematic tastes (they had requested *Forrest Gump* and *Austin Powers*) but the notion that a wedding could serve as occasion to replenish one's DVD collection in the first place.

The discomfort that surrounds the issue of the bridal registry seems to crystallize what is most unsettling about the Bridezilla culture of the contemporary wedding—that the principles of consumerism have taken up seats at the banquet table. This is not to suggest that guests necessarily resent giving gifts. The impulse is a response to what is at a wedding's core, the official establishment of a new family, and this is an impulse that may be felt no less by the friends of Donald Trump than by the friends of newlyweds of lesser means. But what is problematic about the contemporary wedding registry is the way in which it has become the most expressive articulation of a sense of bridal entitlement—an entitlement that not only belongs to the most egregious of Bridezillas but of which all brides are encouraged, by the wedding industry, to partake. "If only the guest list were as easy as the registry list" reads an advertisement for Bloomingdale's bridal registry—a witty observation, but one that depends for its humor upon an understanding of the registry as a form of licensed covetousness, an opportunity to see what degree of acquisitiveness one can get away with.

The covetousness represented, however, is not just that of the couple: It is that of Bloomingdale's, which, like all the retailers against which it competes, has an enormous investment in encouraging in the bride and groom the most vivid fantasies of a domestic bliss that is fully equipped with cookware, ski equipment, and whatever else their hearts desire. And this is also a way in which the contemporary wedding registry conforms to the principles of Bridezilla culture: that behind the apparent acquisitiveness of the bride and groom there looms the boundless acquisitiveness of the corporations that are urging them to express their material desires in the first place.

The first wedding registry was established by Marshall Field's in Chicago in 1924; but the bride had been identified as a customer most worthy of attention since the department store itself was conceived, toward the end of the nineteenth century. The advent of the department store signaled a shift in the culture of shopping. Instead of a harried search for necessities, shopping became a leisure pursuit conducted in palaces of retail that were built using the newest steel-frame-and-stone-construction techniques, were equipped with greenhouses and restaurants, and that offered, for the first time, a multiplicity of goods available under one roof: everything from bedsteads to books to rugs to coats to—in the pet department of Siegel-Cooper's in New York—tropical fish, monkeys, and lion cubs.

The department-store magnates realized that a wedding presented an unusual opportunity, and responded accordingly. Wanamaker's in Philadelphia presented in January 1908 an innovative two-week-long event called "The

Brides' Jubilee," an account of which was given in the trade journal *Merchants Record and Show Window*. "The name suggests a sale of bridal outfits, but it is surprising how many things were made to come under this heading," the magazine reported. Each of the store's thirty-three display windows was filled with wedding-themed merchandise, and a tableau was set up in the Costume Salon of the store showing a bride surrounded by her four bridesmaids and a maid of honor "exquisitely gowned in the latest fashion." Another display in the furnishings department featured "a completely furnished home for $5,000." On the store's basement level, a sample kitchen had been constructed, where, as a Wanamaker's advertisement read "Special instruction is given both in morning & afternoon sessions on *the first principles of cooking & the use of cooking utensils & gas ranges.*" The store even proposed the appropriate brand of upright piano for a bride, though what might make one musical instrument more fitting for a marital home than another is hard to imagine. "The whole store is surcharged with wedding vibrations" the Wanamaker's advertisement read, and those vibrations were surely enhanced by the organist who was stationed in the store's grand court to play wedding marches as an accompaniment to the shoppers' progress through the aisles.

By the 1930s, the department stores had launched bridal salons that sold wedding dresses to affluent and aspiring clients. (They could be staffed, too, by members of the social elite: B. Altman, in New York City, launched its bridal salon in 1927 under the direction of Marie Coudert Brennig, the daughter of a baron and the niece of Condé Nast.) But selling dresses, though it was an important specialty niche, was never the main point of the department stores' interest in the bridal customer. The store owners realized that a bride who was happy with the service she received while buying her dress would return to the store to shop for herself and her new family, and it was the job of the saleswoman in the bridal department "to send away the little bride-elect so satisfied that she'll be a charge customer in your store for life," as *Independent Woman* reported in 1939. The important thing—then as now—was to turn the bride into a permanent consumer. Macy's, the magazine noted, had even gone so far as to hire a consultant "who is stationed in the bride's shop, not to sell wedding apparel, but store services at the exact psychological moment when the about-to-be householder is ready to plan her kitchen, dining-room, or drawing-room facilities."

By the 1950s, the notion that it might fall to the guests at a wedding to equip the bride's kitchen and dining room by giving household items as gifts was becoming well established. *Brides* commissioned a survey of gift-giving habits in 1958 which indicated that half of all brides were indicating their preferences to friends and family, either by direct instruction or by the drawing up of a registry list at a local store. By the fifties, after all, there were so many more gifts to give. In the wake of the Second World War, with marriage rates booming and the GI Bill providing low-interest loans for young couples to purchase houses in suburban tracts, manufacturers had a new customer base for a plethora of new domestic products and electrical gadgets. "The U.S. bridal market represents an *immediate* sales potential of over 1 1/2 billion dollars for home furnishings and household equipment each year, as well as an opportunity to *presell* young couples in terms of additional purchases of these basic items within 2 to 3 years after marriage," reported National Analysts, Inc., which conducted the 1958 *Brides* survey. The *Brides* reader at the time of the survey was about twice as likely as the average bride to specify which brand, color, or pattern of flatware, fine china, or vacuum cleaner she wanted—evidence that the magazine's advertisers had reached their targets effectively.

The survey was designed to show advertisers that the women they were reaching through the pages of *Brides* had much more on their minds than gowns and veils. The American bride was, the survey showed, a very good investment for advertising dollars. She was better educated than the average American woman: Nearly 30 percent of U.S. brides had attended college, as opposed to 12.8 percent of all American women aged twenty-five or older. (Among readers of *Brides*, the figure was 50 percent.) She was also more likely to have a job than the average American woman: Seventy percent of U.S. brides were employed at the time of marriage, while among U.S. women in general only 34 percent were employed. She had savings—a median of $464 per couple at the time of marriage—and was willing to spend: The average cost of a honeymoon trip was $237 per couple. She was young—the median age was twenty—and most exciting of all for the retailers of plates, silverware, and other household items was the fact that 83 percent of brides would, upon marriage, start housekeeping in their own quarters rather than doubling up with their parents or in-laws.

The new tradition of the wedding registry did not languish in the sixties and seventies, in spite of the advent of what was called "the new wedding," influenced by the mores of the counterculture. According to Marcia Seligson in her book about the wedding industry, *The Eternal Bliss Machine*, which was published in 1973, $200 million was being spent on wedding gifts each year, and the bride was embarking upon married life with 120 major new products to her name, not all of them woks or subscriptions to *The Whole Earth Catalog*.

Today's wedding-registry business is more elaborate than ever before, particularly since couples no longer need register in person with a local department store but have access to the infinite warehouses of online retailers. More than forty years after *Brides* commissioned the survey referred to earlier, *Modern Bride* magazine commissioned the research firm Roper Starch to conduct a similar survey of the shopping and registry intentions of the bride-to-be compared with those of the unbetrothed, the results of which were conveyed in a report, published in 2000, entitled "Your New $100 Billion Customer: The Engaged Woman." The engaged woman was by now a very different creature—assumed to be coming to her marriage having already established a home and a career—but nonetheless she saw her marriage as an opportunity to acquire the equipment of domestic life. Fifty-six percent of the respondents in the survey who were already engaged said they expected to receive gifts of fine crystal within the next six months, compared with 1 percent of single women. Sixty-nine percent of engaged women expected to be given bath towels, compared to 3 percent of the unattached. Fifty-nine percent of engaged women agreed with the statement "Having a coordinated look for my bedding is important," while a mere 34 percent of the unbetrothed assented to the proposition.

Becoming engaged was an occasion for self-improvement as well as home improvement. "Having found the right man in no way lessens an engaged woman's focus on looking/feeling her best," the study reported. "In the past 12 months, they are more likely to have gone on a diet, started a new exercise routine, attended a tanning session, purchased more expensive cosmetics, used a home tooth whitener, and tried a new method of birth control." In fact, single women were reported to outspend their engaged sisters in only two areas: They bought more pagers, and they were more likely to have changed their hair color in the past six months. The picture of the unattached life evoked by the survey is not a happy one: lonely nights passed between mismatched sheets, after evenings spent in the bathroom with a bottle of Miss Clairol, waiting for a beep on the pager.

"I think today's entertainer is a resourceful entertainer," Colin Cowie told me when I visited him. His apartment, which he shares with his boyfriend and business partner, Stuart Brownstein, serves as both home and office, and is on a high floor of a converted loft building. The front door opens into an expansive entertaining space, decorated in shades of white and gray, with low, modernist couches, a gleaming grand piano, and artworks by celebrated contemporary artists, including Vanessa Beecroft and Richard Serra. "It's more important that we live than that we do things perfectly right," said Cowie, who was born in Zambia and grew up in South Africa (he is now an American citizen). When he pronounced the word *live*, it came out sounding like "luff."

Luffstyle, Cowie contends, is what today's weddings are all about. "Your wedding is not just another big party; it is your opportunity to make a statement of style to your family and friends and your new family and friends," he said. "So everything you do should be an expression of self. There are no rules today in weddings, so my advice to the bride is, be guided by your own sense of style. So long as you are not offending anyone and your personality is shining through, then embrace that idea to the fullest."

Cowie moved to Los Angeles in the mid-eighties, and got his big break in 1989 when he was seated next to the wife of the president of Playboy Enterprises at a luncheon just six weeks before Hugh Hefner was to be wed for the second time, to Kimberley Conrad, the 1988 Playmate of the Year. Cowie was hired to plan the wedding, which took place at the Playboy Mansion. "I kept it very English," he said. "I made it very grand. They insisted on doing buffets, so I turned the buffets into art pieces, with the waiters changing their uniforms and the flowers changing between courses. You walked upstairs to be served, and then went downstairs and there was dancing, and then when the next course came the decor was completely different." For the caviar course, tables were draped with purple orchids; for the meat course of boneless baby lamb, New York steak, grilled baby chicken, and haricots verts, red satin and gold braiding was substituted: "So food and theater and art all came together."

That wedding established Cowie. "Directly after that, I did my first big million-dollar wedding," he said. "It was for the Marshall Field's fortune— Ted Field." Celebrity weddings and parties followed. "I have worked with Bruce and Demi, and Tom and Nicole, and Seinfeld, and Michael Jordan, and Oprah Winfrey, and John Travolta, and all these people," he said. For the wedding of Don Henley, which is featured in *Colin Cowie Weddings*, Emeril Lagasse planned the menu, Tony Bennett played a set, and Sting, Bruce

Springsteen, Billy Joel, and Sheryl Crow got up to sing. (The book also includes weddings of clients who are not famous but merely rich, like the bride who wanted to turn her family's horse ranch into a set from the movie *The Age of Innocence*, with thousands of roses around the fireplace where the vows were exchanged and a seven-tiered cake ornamented with gold leaf.) Commissioning a Colin Cowie wedding, Cowie said, was comparable to buying haute couture: "Like going to Paris and having Saint Laurent make the gown for you."

Cowie's venture with JCPenney was intended to bring his sense of wedding style to the masses. "We can have brands coexist in different parts of the marketplace today," he said. "Years ago, you had to pick one place and stay in one place, but now I can have my haute couture line and my prêt-à-porter line." For JCPenney Cowie had produced a wedding planning guide that was sent in a ring-binder to every bride who signed up to register for wedding gifts, as well as four seasonal wedding-style guides containing advice floral, culinary, and sartorial. The winter bride was urged to incorporate berries and fruit into her centerpieces, and to remember to wear closed-toe shoes; while the spring bride should consider sending out chartreuse- and saffron-colored invitations and serving pea soup garnished with a lump of crab salad, thereby taking the soup "from drab to fab." Cowie was pictured in each guide dressed in his own seasonally appropriate wear: a purple shirt for fall, a daring, bright-red crushed-velvet shirt for winter.

Cowie explained that he and JCPenney had also gone into the business of supplying products to be used at the wedding itself, including tableware, stemware, and table linens—all of which were also eminently suitable to be included in a wedding-registry wish list. "We have the 'Wedding in a Box,'" he told me. "Invariably when you go to a rental company, or you go to a banquet hall of a restaurant, you get a round white table with ten chairs. We offer a gorgeous hand-embroidered, beaded overlay in one of our signature colors, like eggplant or amethyst, and you get ten votive candles, and you get a gorgeous glass bowl for your flowers, in amethyst, and you get ten beautiful amethyst napkins. So you have the ability to give instant style to your table." He planned to make it possible for a bride of modest means to—in a favorite expression—"Colinize" her entire wedding.

"I am moving into bedding, into bathroom, into kitchen; I am going to do the whole home thing," he told me. "To me, it is all about living, and the wedding just gets you down the aisle. Now you have registered for all this stuff, you have to live. We need to empower that person and tell them how to live, and how to use the product. And we have to sell them the product, and design great products for them."

Being able to select and purchase bedsheets with a high enough thread count may be a rather degraded notion of empowerment, but Cowie's meaning was clear. A wedding is an expression of a lifestyle, he argued—the one you have, or the one you want to have; and the same is true of a wedding registry. Both present an opportunity to express one's taste and sense of style, preferably through the use of products that express Cowie's sense of taste and style.

Cowie was utterly charming—the kind of guy it would be great fun to hang out with at a party, even if you couldn't actually commission him to orchestrate any party at which he might hang out—and his high-low sensibility is what people in the fashion business call very modern. Certainly he struck a very different note from that sounded by other players in the wedding industry: Unlike Vera Wang, who had spoken at the Wedding March on Madison about the "mad, divine obsession of weddings," and unlike Korri McFann at Disney with her talk of "fairy-tale magic," he seemed completely unconcerned with making avowals about the romance of weddings, or about the glories of marriage thereafter. Perhaps this was because Cowie, as a gay man in a long-term relationship, knew that wedding ceremonies were not necessary to secure a partnership, and provided no guarantee of security in any case.

Or perhaps he really wasn't interested in weddings except as an "opportunity to make a statement of style to your family and friends," as he had said earlier. A wedding as a statement of style struck me as a pretty impoverished notion: Surely weddings are a statement of much more than that? But it sounded as if Cowie, for professional purposes at least, had determined that personal style was what weddings were about, rather than being about one of the other meanings one might give to a wedding: the merging of families, the conforming to cultural mores, the adherence to religious rites, or even the expression of love. These meanings, you might argue, serve to integrate a wedding into life, grounding it in social practices and giving it a relevance beyond a couple's choices of color schemes or cocktail recipes; but in Cowie's vision, lifestyle—*luff*style—had trumped life.

Cowie was entirely unsentimental, not just about the business of weddings but about weddings themselves, and the marriages they inaugurated. When our conversation moved off the subject immediately at hand—Cowie's business ventures—and into areas in which he did not have a marketing message to deliver, his comments about marriage were strikingly negative for someone whose livelihood and reputation depend upon the institution.

"The whole ideology of marriage has changed," he said. "Our social responsibility has fallen by the wayside, and we have gotten way too goal-oriented and way too selfish. So in many instances, when people are married and have a career and have kids, they get to this age where they say, 'This isn't what I signed up for; I am moving on. This is not what I was expecting.' " Women are as faithless as men, he said. "A lot of women today will use a man just to have a child. They'd rather be married and divorced with a kid at forty-two than still waiting for it to happen."

I asked Cowie what the success rate of the weddings he had planned was, and his voice lowered to a sardonic purr, somewhere between Bogart and Bacall. "Sweetheart, I really don't care," he said. "I just get 'em down the aisle."

· · ·

When, three years after his initial hiring by JCPenney, Cowie's contract with the retailer was not renewed, I wondered whether Cowie's views about marriage had had anything to do, obliquely, with the ending of that business alliance. I couldn't know: Cowie wasn't talking, and JCPenney's public-relations department said only that Cowie's line of products "did not resonate with JCPenney shoppers as well as we had hoped," as Cowie's brick-and-camel-colored Medina comforters and pillow shams languished in the store's discount bins. But it seemed to me possible that, on some unspoken level, Cowie had proven too cynical about marriage, even for an industry in which cynicism about the business of brides is widespread and in which the bride's status as what Cowie had called a "slam dunk" is the received wisdom.

Certainly, JCPenney's next move in trying to secure its share of the valuable wedding-registry market suggested that it wanted to project a wholesome, optimistic view of marriage. After Cowie left, the company appointed LeAnn Rimes, the country music singer, and her dancer husband, Dean Sheremet, to be the new faces of the bridal registry—perhaps a better fit for a company based in Plano, Texas, than a Manhattan-dwelling wedding planner. (In the fall of 2006, Cowie signed a new deal himself: this time with Wal-Mart, to produce a line of holiday housewares and home decor, unrelated to the company's bridal registry.) Within a few months the black-and-white photo spreads in JCPenney's advertising inserts started featuring "wedding pictures"—restaged some four years after the actual event—of Rimes and Sheremet.

The pair were shown in a series of faux-candid shots enacting the kind of down-home but aesthetically refined celebration to which JCPenney brides might well aspire. One picture showed a meal served outside on a long table set with abundant flowers; in another Rimes and Sheremet sat on a wooden couch under brilliant sunshine, about to exchange a kiss. Rimes, who was nineteen when she married in 2002, had blond curls framing her face and wore a strapless gown, while Sheremet, who was twenty-one when they married, had a Brad Pitt hairline and wore a tux with an open-collared shirt. (Their actual wedding, featured in *In Style Weddings*, had conformed to the "simple elegance" formula, according to Rimes's wedding planner, Jeffrey Best, who is one of Colin Cowie's West Coast rivals. In their case it was a simple elegance that called for a cake decorated with thirty-five dozen red roses, a Vera Wang gown, and a string of a dozen half-carat diamonds sewn into Rimes's hair.)

The message conveyed by the advertisement was simple and elegant, too: "Marriage joins together two hearts, two souls, two different sets of dishware," read the copy on one page. "True love, like a cast iron skillet, should be able to stand the test of time," it read on another. With the lightest of ironies, a promise was made that marital happiness inhered in kitchen items. It was, though, the very lightest of ironies, since the promise of the photos was that married life—like that actually experienced by Rimes and Sheremet—could remain a perpetual wedding celebration, with kisses exchanged on a couch set with beaded cushions available from JCPenney.

Six

God and the Details

"I am fond of saying that coming to me is like going to a Chinese restaurant: Choose one item from columns A, B, and C," Joyce Gioia, a freelance wedding minister, told me one bright, hot Saturday morning, as she swung her rental car out of the Princeton Junction parking lot where she had picked me up and headed toward the Molly Pitcher Inn, a hotel on the New Jersey Shore where she was to perform a wedding that day. Gioia was a diminutive, attractive woman in her middle years, with dewy porcelain skin, curled hair tinted to a dark mahogany, and big eyes ringed with black liner. As the car's global-positioning system issued robotic instructions, she took one hand from the steering wheel, opened her handbag, and drew out a large fistful of assorted vitamin pills, which she dumped into her lap, catching them in the silken folds of her royal blue dress, then began gulping them down with the help of swigs from a juice bottle. There were capsules filled with gleaming golden liquid, others stuffed with what looked like sawdust, mysterious white tablets of all sizes, and one enormous black bolus that looked like something a veterinarian might force down the gullet of a sick horse.

Having learned from Colin Cowie that a wedding should be an expression of a couple's lifestyle, and having learned at the Business of Brides conference about the "spin on tradition" that characterized the contemporary wedding—as well as having been exposed, both by Beverly Clark and by Disney's Fairy Tale Weddings program, to the contemporary nuptial idiom of the traditionalesque—I began to wonder how those elements would be expressed not just in the wedding reception—the party part of a wedding—but in the marriage ceremony that lay at the wedding's heart.

Joyce Gioia, I suspected, might be able to provide some answers. Gioia is a self-described multifaith minister who has been performing weddings since the late 1980s. She is featured in "The Knot Guide to Wedding Vows and Traditions," which says she is "known for her personalized candle rituals" and includes a honey ceremony of Gioia's device, in which a bride and groom dab little fingers dipped in honey upon each other's tongue.

Gioia has conducted all sorts of unconventional wedding ceremonies. There was a wedding of two Muslims of Indian descent who both grew up in Africa—the bride in Tanzania, and the groom in Uganda—that combined traditions such as the decoration of the bride's hands with elaborate henna patterns with more modern practices such as a reception in an upscale Indian restaurant. For the wedding of a member of an old-timers' baseball team that was conducted on the ball field of Pelham Bay Park in the Bronx— the groom's teammates stood in two lines from second base to the pitcher's mound and held up their bats in an archway to form the aisle—Gioia wore an umpire's uniform and concluded the ceremony by asking the guests to hold hands and sing "Take Me Out to the Ball Game." Along with another wedding minister, Gioia has also devised a divorce ceremony for couples who wish to mark the end of a marriage with something more than the writing of checks to lawyers. (The ceremony typically includes the returning of the wedding rings and a ritualistic burning of an item that was meaningful for the couple, the marriage certificate being a popular choice.)

"I create a wedding that is uniquely that couple, and I don't think I have ever performed two weddings that are alike," Gioia explained to me as she drove toward the wedding. "The new thing is options marketing, giving people more options, which I have been doing for years." Just a few weeks earlier, she had officiated at a medieval-themed wedding at Castle McCulloch—actually a restored gold-mining factory—near Greensboro, North Carolina, where she lives. "The groom was in chain mail, and the bride was in a medieval dress, and the groomsmen were in period costume, like the Three Musketeers," Gioia said. "I wore my old robe, which has a hood. It was just wonderful."

Her field of specialization is conducting the weddings of couples who come from two different cultural or religious backgrounds, she explained. Over the years she has amassed a considerable computerized database of prayers, readings, and bits of ceremonial business, drawn from sources that range from the Bible to the works of Marianne Williamson, that she cuts and pastes as required. "Generally, when a couple gets to me they are looking to marry in a way that honors both of their religious backgrounds," she said. "So I bring together the liturgy, or whatever the religion is, and I fix it up so that it is not offensive. The net is that I get to keep the languaging without having all the religiosity." Such sensitivity does not come cheap: Gioia's standard fee for a wedding in New York, she told me, was a thousand dollars per ceremony—twice the fee of some of her competitors. "I do more customization than other ministers, and I have most of the wedding committed to memory," she said. "It is very unusual for me to complete a wedding and not for one person to come up and say, 'That was the most beautiful wedding I have ever been to.'" She has delivered benedictions in about fifteen different languages including French, Spanish, German, Latin, Greek, Hebrew, Cantonese, Mandarin, and Ibo. After the wedding is over, she gives a signed, dated copy of the ceremony to the couple: "It's kind of a value-added," she said.

Weddings, as her business-school lexicon suggests, are only a part of Gioia's professional life. She was, she explained, also the president of The Herman Group, a management consultancy that she ran with her third husband, Roger Herman—who, like Gioia, went by the distinctive professional appellation of "strategic business futurist." When she is not marrying people Gioia travels around the country to business conventions and seminars to give talks about how to Make Work Meaningful or how to Create Your Future; The Herman Group also issues The Herman Trend Alert, a fascinating weekly e-mail advisory sent to twenty-nine thousand subscribers. Past topics include "Women Will Be More Desirable," about businesses' cultivation of female employees with flexible hours and other family-friendly policies, and "Pet-Centric Architecture"—about windows being placed at doggie level in new buildings.

When it comes to her ministerial vocation, Gioia's approach might be characterized as that of a strategic spiritual futurist. Gioia is Jewish by birth (her maiden name was Kaplan; Gioia is the euphonious legacy of her second husband), but spiritually she leans more toward the New Age than the Old Testament. She acquired her master's degrees in counseling and in theology from the New Seminary, an institute in Manhattan that was founded by Joseph Gelberman, a rabbi with yogic inclinations, upon the ruling principle of honoring all belief systems equally. Gioia has an affect of corporate briskness that sits in odd contrast to her spiritual tenets, which include the conviction that the wearing of a watch saps your energy. "People say after my wedding ceremonies, 'I want to attend your services, where is your church?'" she told me. "I want to say, 'I don't have one. It is against my religion.'" Gioia was still working her way through the stash of pills in her lap while we spoke, and one capsule filled with a honey-colored liquid spilled out of her palm and rolled down the side of the car seat. She looked at me and said, "If I dropped it, I wasn't supposed to take it."

We arrived at the Molly Pitcher Inn—a hotel built in the 1920s overlooking the Navesink River in Red Bank, New Jersey—and, after Gioia had introduced herself to the groom, we went up to the bride's room. The bride was almost ready. From the neck up, she looked as if she had stepped from a bridal portrait that could have been taken in any decade of the past fifty years, with polished, pretty makeup and blond hair swept up into a twist and pinned with a short veil. The rest of her was less conventional in appearance: She wore a white strapless bra and gray sweatpants, the waistband of which was pulled down below a clearly pregnant belly, which was very tan and decorated with a gold belly-button ring. She looked healthy and happy and absolutely beautiful, if a bit hot.

Gioia sorted through her props, which included candles and a foil-wrapped package that contained a glass for a glass-breaking ceremony (actually a lightbulb, a substitution that removed the risk of glass shards stabbing the sole of anyone's foot but still provided a satisfying popping sound upon shattering). After changing into her long white ceremonial robe, Gioia descended to the wedding site, a sun-baked rooftop deck overlooking the water. She lit a candle which she would refer to during the ceremony as the "eternal light," and advised the photographer about forthcoming photo opportunities. Guests started to arrive, some in suits and some in Bermuda shorts, and took up their seats, squinting in the sun at the floral arbor under which the ceremony would be conducted. Eventually the bride descended to meet the groom blooming in her white maternity bridal gown.

I stood to the side, by the railings of the deck, and listened as Gioia worked her way through the service, which comprised a disorienting volley of symbolic rituals. The groom was Jewish and the bride Christian, and Gioia alluded to both of these heritages, with a quasi-Christian prayer calling upon the Divine Spirit—form and gender unspecified—to stay by their side in the days ahead; a wine ceremony, for which Gioia gave the blessing in Hebrew and in English; and an exchange of vows that drew loosely upon the vows in the Book of Common Prayer, in which the groom expressed his choice of the bride as "my friend, my love, the mother of our children," the last eliciting an indulgent chuckle from the assembled.

But there were also rituals that were neither Christian nor Jewish but rather nonspecifically spiritual in affect. Gioia performed her celebrated candle ceremony—the same one that appeared in "The Knot Guide to Wedding Vows and Traditions"—which was a very theatrical variation on the Unity Candle ceremony that has become a popular part of many contemporary weddings. (The ritual surrounding the Unity Candle—actually two slender tapers and one thicker pillar, which are usually set in a decorative tripartite candelabra—can vary, but most commonly the outer, slender candles are lit at the beginning of the marriage service by the mothers of the bride and groom, and then, at some point during the ceremony, the bride and groom use their individual tapers simultaneously to light the single large candle, either snuffing out the smaller candles or keeping them alight.) Gioia introduced her variation on the candle ceremony by saying, "Ancient sages tell us that for each of us, there is a candle, a symbol of our own light, but that no one can kindle his or her own candle. Each of us needs someone else to kindle it for us." The bride and groom each lit a candle from the "eternal light," merged them into one flame, and then drew them apart again to symbolize the nature of married life, with the photographer snapping vigorously throughout.

There was a New Age sermon, which advised the bride and groom of the necessity of recognizing their own unique and special individuality before they might achieve the transcendence of ego required for marital harmony.

Gioia also recited something called the Apache Indian Prayer. "Now you will feel no rain, for each of you will be shelter for the other; now you will feel no cold, for each of you will be warmth for the other," she intoned, as the guests sweltered upon the unshaded deck. "Now you are two bodies, but there is only one life before you."

Back in the hotel room after the ceremony was over, I checked the time—the whole wedding ceremony had taken about eighteen minutes—and Gioia offered to show me how my watch was sapping my energy. "Take off your watch and stick your stronger arm out," she said. I did so, holding my left arm perpendicular to my body. "I am going to unzip your aura," Gioia said, and, bending down at my left foot, she made a zipping motion up the front of my body and along the length of my arm. Then she pushed down on my out-stretched arm, which gave a little under the force.

"Now hold your watch in your right hand," she said. I did so, and this time when she pressed down on my left arm it gave way much further. Next, Gioia reached into the sports bra she was wearing under her long white robe and withdrew a small object: a copper coil set into plastic, which she gave me to hold in my right fist instead of the watch. It was a little warm. She pressed down on my left arm again, which this time gave hardly at all under the force of her push.

She took back the coil—it was called a Q-link, she said—and tucked it into her bra again with an inscrutable smile. Hours later, at home, I realized with a start that she had neglected to zip up my aura again, and I had been walking around with it open all that time.

The wedding Gioia had allowed me to observe was affecting in a joyful, bois-terous way—the bride punched the air gleefully as she made her way back up the aisle with her husband—and the bride's pregnancy served as a hearty antidote to the precepts of Bridezilla culture, a reminder that a wedding is

not really about coordinating one's napkins to match one's floral arrangements. But even though I had been moved by the ceremony, I came away feeling glutted by the ceremonial variety that Gioia had offered. The metaphor
of the Chinese menu didn't seem quite right to me: This wedding was more
like a plate spilling over with pickings from an international buffet at an all-
inclusive resort hotel, where lunch might consist of a slice of lasagna, a ladle-
ful of goulash, and a couple of pieces of nori-wrapped California roll on the
side, with a hot fudge sundae to follow up.

I also wondered how many ceremonies from different sources could be
piled up before they started to cancel one another out. Christians and Jews
marry each other in contemporary America, of course, and so do couples of
other religious persuasions; and it is understandable that they would want to
do so in a way that paid tribute to the traditions of each culture. This is true
even when the wedding amounts to a violation of the historical beliefs and
practices of the traditions in question: How one honors all belief systems
equally—the credo of Joseph Gelberman's New Seminary—when to do so is to
violate the First Commandment of the Judeo-Christian Bible is a question
perhaps only answerable by someone equipped with both a rabbinical education and an ability to perform yogic contortions. But Gioia's wedding
ceremony went beyond the attempt to honor the bride and groom's backgrounds equally. It incorporated rituals, such as the candle ceremony, that
seemed to have come largely from Gioia's own imagination, and it drew upon
traditions—or the semblance of traditions—from cultures to which neither
bride nor bridegroom belonged, such as the Apache wedding prayer.

In fact, neither ritual was quite what it seemed. Although Gioia had spoken of the wisdom of "ancient sages" when she introduced her candle ceremony, the use of the so-called Unity Candle in wedding ceremonies appears
to date back only to the mid-1960s, according to a PhD thesis investigating
its history and use by Charles William Salisbury, a ministerial candidate at

Lancaster Theological Seminary. While Salisbury found no smoking Unity Candle that would determine decisively whence the custom originated, he did raise several tantalizing hypotheses of its provenance of varying likelihood: that it may have been invented by the floral or greeting-card industries; that it may have gained widespread currency after an appearance on a daytime soap opera (with a reported but unconfirmed sighting on an episode of *The Young and the Restless* in the mid-seventies); that it may have been started by the hippie countercultural movement. Salisbury raised the possibility that its use in a newly popular "handfasting" ritual, whereby the hands of the bride and groom are tied together to symbolize their union, actually derived from pagan origins; but he was unable to determine whether the neo-pagans got the idea for using candles from their pagan precursors, or whether they picked it up from daytime television themselves.

The Unity Candle ceremony is often ascribed to Catholic ritual—this is how it is categorized in "The Knot Guide to Wedding Vows and Traditions"— but this is a misapprehension. In fact, Catholic clergy have been particularly vexed by requests from couples wishing to incorporate candle ceremonies into the church's rites of marriage, which individual priests are prohibited from customizing. The Catholic authorities in the United States have gone so far as to order an investigation of the practice by the Secretariat of the Bishops Committee on the Liturgy, which is based in Washington. In the early nineties the Secretariat issued a statement on the candle's use that is a masterpiece of clerical deconstruction. Within the Catholic liturgy, the authors explained, a lighted candle always represents the light of Christ, and is lit constantly throughout the service as a symbol of Christ's presence. But the meaning of the three lights of the unity candle, which are variously unlit, lit, and snuffed out at different points in the service, is much murkier. "If the two smaller candles are meant to represent the individual baptized Christians entering this marriage, should not that symbolization be made explicit, such as, by the bride and groom each carrying their candle in the entrance procession?" the authors asked. The larger candle was even more problematic for the Secretariat. If it was supposed to represent Christ, then shouldn't it be ignited at the beginning of the service, rather than halfway through? And, the authors reasonably asked, "If the lighted candle does not represent Christ, what does it symbolize? The couple? If so, it seems to be at variance with liturgical tradition."

The "Apache Indian Prayer" is not all it appeared to be, either. The prayer is reproduced, with slight variation, in several wedding-planning handbooks and on innumerable Web sites, and is in wide and popular use. (It even acquired a celebrity sheen in 2003, when Russell Crowe and his bride, Danielle Spencer, used it for their wedding on Crowe's Australian ranch, where it served as a counterpoint to the cavalcade of leather-clad bikers who accompanied the bridal limousine.) But so far as I can determine from research in libraries, speaking with scholars of Apache culture, and with actual keepers of Apache culture, the prayer appears to be a poetic fiction. While Apaches have extensive rituals to celebrate, for example, a teenage girl's coming of age, it turns out they have very little in the way of wedding ritual. The classic text on Apache customs, *An Apache Life-Way*, by Morris Opler, which was published in 1941, has no reference to wedding-day rituals at all, save the remark that Apache marriages are begun without very much in the way of ceremony beyond the giving of gifts by the groom to his new wife's family and the construction of a new home for the couple.

The so-called Apache prayer is sometimes referred to in wedding-planning sources as a Navajo wedding prayer; and unlike the Apaches, the Navajo do have a wedding ceremony. But this prayer isn't part of it. The central ritual of a Navajo wedding is the blessing by a medicine man of a bowl of blue corn-meal mush from which the bride and groom eat, thereby incorporating the commitment of marriage irreversibly into their bodies. The concept of the unification of two lives into one that is so moving a part of the

Apache Indian Prayer is alien to the Navajo way of thinking about marriage, in which the bride and groom are perceived as continuing on the separate paths of their lives even after coming to live together in one home.

It was a Native American, Ramon Riley, the cultural resource director of the White Mountain Apache Cultural Center, in Fort Apache, Arizona, who pointed me toward the apparent source of the Apache wedding prayer. "It's from a movie called *Broken Arrow*, starring James Stewart and Deborah Paget," he told me. The movie was shot in the White Mountains, and starred Apaches as extras, but the so-called Apache prayer, Riley said, "was written by non-Indians, who are not even getting advice from the horse's mouth, and they are always incorrect."

The movie is a quasi-historical tale of the American West that won an Academy Award for its screenplay in 1950, and was adapted from the bestselling historical novel *Blood Brothers*, by Elliott Arnold. Based upon a true story, the movie concerns the friendship between Tom Jeffords, a frontiersman who is played by Jimmy Stewart, and the Indian chief Cochise, played by Jeff Chandler. *Broken Arrow* has been praised by cultural historians for the sensitivity and faithfulness of its portrayal of Apache Indians, whose earlier representation in Hollywood productions had been far from accurate or flattering.

In fact, the only part of the movie that comes in for much criticism on grounds of inaccuracy is a wedding ceremony that is performed by Cochise to inaugurate the—entirely fictional—marriage between Tom Jeffords and Sonseeahray, a Native American maiden played by the sixteen-year-old Deborah Paget. (The love story was an invention to appeal to mass American tastes: Elliott Arnold, in his introduction to *Blood Brothers*, wrote, "I have taken a writer's liberty and imagined that such a wedding took place.") In the course of the ceremony Cochise cuts incisions on the fingers of Stewart and Paget, mingles their blood, and stoically intones the verses about the rain and the cold. Thereupon the pair mount a single white horse and gallop off in the direction of the ceremonial teepee that Paget has described earlier in the film as being readied for their "honeymoon," as if it were a hotel suite with a heart-shaped bathtub of the sort found in resorts around the time of the movie's release. Of the whole performance John E. O'Connor, the author of a book called *The Hollywood Indian: Stereotypes of Native Americans in Films*, wrote scathingly, "The moving marriage ceremony and wedding night rituals portrayed in the film are Hollywood fantasy."

If the Apache prayer came from popular American rather than Native American culture, it wouldn't be the first time Gioia had drawn upon the movies for her ceremonies: She told me she had one invocation she regularly used in her ceremonies—"It is in this spirit that I welcome you and greet you"—which she picked up from a movie just because she liked the sound of it. Wherever their words originated, it was clear that Gioia believed the kind of wedding ceremonies she conducted had the power to be much more meaningful than those whose every moment was scripted according to long-standing cultural or religious convention.

This, it turned out, was the form that her own first wedding, in 1970, had taken. That had been held at the Roosevelt hotel in her hometown of New Orleans with three hundred guests—"There was a bride's cake and a groom's cake, greenery everywhere, and a chuppah the size of half of the audience at the wedding we just went to," she told me as we drove from the Molly Pitcher Inn—and a ceremony conducted by the rabbi she had known since childhood. I asked Gioia if she thought the couples whose ceremonies she performs miss out at all by not being married by an authority figure from within a familiar community, as she had been.

"Yes and no," she said. "Yes, in the sense that you are not getting the same sense of stability and security and traditionalism as you do when you are growing up with something. But also you are not getting the traditional, 'This is the way we are doing the wedding, and you don't have any say.' My couples get to give an input into their wedding." In Gioia's vision, the wedding was an expression of the couple's inner spirituality, rather than of their submission to the spiritual authority of a larger institution. It was also an expression of their taste when it came to religious ritual—their selection among the array of elements Gioia could offer, all of which she would perform with the solemn affect of the absolute, no matter which they chose, and no matter the origin or the authenticity of the element in question.

As we drove along, Gioia told me more about her own marital history—her wedding to her second husband had been co-performed by Rabbi Gelberman and a Catholic priest, and with her third husband she had actually had two wedding ceremonies nearly three years apart, the first a purely spiritual one ("We wanted to get married in the eyes of God but couldn't justify paying thousands more to the federal government in taxes"), and the second one, after Roger Herman had suffered a heart attack, with paperwork. ("Roger said, 'I want to make it legal. I don't care what it costs. There's a difference between someone you're living with and someone you're married to.'") I asked Gioia how her own history of broken nuptial commitments affected her perspective as she invited couples to pledge themselves to each other for life. "I send them on and I bless them to the degree I can," she said. "I feel that when couples come to me, there's a reason. It's not my job to talk them out of marriage. There are lessons they are supposed to learn together."

It was a surprisingly modest account of her role as the legal and religious authority to whom couples had entrusted this momentous responsibility, but it made sense. Gioia was a minister without a church, and without a tradition. Her wedding ceremonies sought to honor the traditional, but what they accomplished was the elevation of the bride and groom, in a celebration of individuality, over the traditions from which they had come. The clients she inducted into marriage exchanged hands and vows in the name of individual freedom, but they did so in the vertiginous absence of an institutional anchor. Once the ceremony was over, they were on their own.

. . .

As a freelance, part-time minister offering an aura of spirituality without the regulations of organized religion, Gioia was meeting a need presented by some among the roughly 40 percent of the American public who are what scholars of religion refer to as "the unchurched," those who have no membership or affiliation with any religious institution. The opportunity presented by this market of brides and grooms has been recognized by all sorts of entrepreneurs, and at the Business of Brides conference in Kansas City, Miriam Juris, a rabbi specializing in interfaith marriage, had advised aspiring wedding planners to be prepared to perform marriages themselves in a pinch, should a minister fail to show up for one reason or another. They could do this by equipping themselves with credentials from the Universal Life Church, a bizarre organization based in Modesto, California, that makes ordination available online to anyone who applies, and makes of them no training requirements. The church, which was founded by a renegade Baptist minister named Kirby Hensley in the 1960s and is now run by his son, Andre Hensley, claims it has enrolled 18 million ministers since its foundation. Ministers ordained by the Universal Life Church can legally perform marriages almost anywhere in the United States without further documentation; they can also, for a fee of five dollars, acquire from the church's headquarters a certificate bearing one of about one hundred alternative religious titles, including Cardinal, Lama, Guru, Friar, Reverend Mother, Swami, Magus, Dervish, High Priestess, Druid, Monk, Baron, Apostle of Humility, Martyr, Goddess, Angel, and Saint.

One multitasking minister I came across was the Reverend Bob Martin, in Waretown, New Jersey, who had the foresight to register the domain name weddingminister.com. When I called Reverend Bob—as he styles himself—he told me that he had a certificate from the Universal Life Church (though he said that he had acquired his ministerial credentials through another institution he declined to name) and said that he offers religious and nonreligious weddings, "instant weddings," and elopements. He told me that his ministry "revolves around the lost souls that flee to church edifices and then are kicked away because they are not a member of the church or they have been married and divorced."

Reverend Bob also turns out to be DJ Bob, the proprietor of A Class Act disc jockey service, in which capacity he has been servicing the wedding market for about twenty years, as well as appearing in 2005 and 2006 as the host of the Mrs. New Jersey America pageant, a role not typically assigned to a man of God. Sometimes, he told me, he serves as both minister and disc jockey at the same wedding, and has a ready answer for any guests who might wonder at the appropriateness of that combination of callings: "I will say to them, do you sing in church? And wasn't Jesus partying for three days at the wedding at Cana? And didn't he turn water into wine to continue the party? Why then can't I be musically inclined and move this party on?" Another hat worn by Reverend Bob is as a dealer of automatic cannons that disperse large volumes of confetti over a dance floor, a party trick even the Cana crowd might have been impressed by. Yet another of his professional incarnations is as Robert James, Magician, in which capacity he offers, according to the A Class Act Web site, "The Best of Magic, Prestidigitation, and Illusion"—a description that seems to capture something essential about his wedding ministry as well.

The notion underlying ministries such as Reverend Bob's or Joyce Gioia's is a familiar one in the contemporary culture of weddings: that a wedding ceremony, like a wedding reception, ought to be an expression of the character of the couple who are getting married, rather than an expression of the character of the institution marrying them. This notion is one that organized religions are wrestling with in their own ways. There are many different institutions, and many characters; the variety of religious persuasions in the United States defies generalization, and so does the variety of religious wedding ceremonies. At a Quaker wedding, there is silent mutual prayer before the bride and groom speak their vows to each other without need for a minister as an intermediary; a Catholic wedding is accompanied, on the contrary, by a lengthy mass. Non-Christian traditions make the range even wider. But even taking into account the breadth of different wedding services that are regularly performed, churches are increasingly faced, on the one hand, with the request of unchurched couples who nonetheless are seeking on their wedding day a little more churchiness than the likes of Reverend Bob can offer, and, on the other hand, with the demands of church members who would like to be able to inject just a smidgen of Reverend Bob into the proceedings.

"Couples and their families seem to think theirs should be a princess wedding replete with celebratory devices," Douglas G. Scott, then the rector of St. Martin's Episcopal Church in Radnor, Pennsylvania, wrote in the pages of *Christianity Today* a few years ago, in response to these emerging demands. "Liturgical accoutrement and even mini-rings for children of a previous union are common. No one throws rice anymore; they release balloons or blow bubbles." Couples, he complained, attempted to secure his services in much the same spirit as they hired a wedding planner or a disc jockey: "They have already been to the florist, the dressmaker, the reception hall, and the caterer," he wrote. "Their meeting with the minister is just another wedding necessity."

The note of frustration sounded by the the Reverend Douglas Scott is not an isolated one. In the late 1990s the Liturgical Commission of the Episcopal Diocese of New York issued a statement outlining its position on appropriate and inappropriate practices during a marriage ceremony, and its list of criticisms and interdictions suggest the problems with which clergy come face-to-face when performing the rites of marriage. "Weddings have recently become very costly undertakings," the commission noted. "In planning weddings, clergy should encourage simplicity and urge the couple to keep costs low so that undue burdens are not placed upon the families, and that

expensive accessories and other events do not overshadow the powerful simplicity of the rite of joining hands and exchanging vows in the setting of the
Church's liturgy."

Among the objects of disapproval were the flashing of cameras from the
pews ("We prefer that all guests concentrate upon participating in the liturgy
and praying for the couple rather than upon anticipating the next photo opportunity"); the inclusion of poetical, devotional, or philosophical readings
("Fine things in their own right, but many of them are not Christian"); cute
toddler ring bearers ("an invitation to disaster"); elaborate floral displays
("While it is important to respect cultural traditions of the community, many
decorations and flowers are, like some music, better suited to the reception
hall than to the church"); and the presence of professional wedding planners
("We suggest that they be forbidden to attend rehearsals and under no circumstances may questions about the liturgy be referred to them"). Similarly
reproachable are some couples' impatience with the fact that certain periods
during the Christian calendar, such as Lent and Advent, are off-limits for
weddings except in an instance of "serious, pressing, compelling pastoral
need" (which does not include, the Commission noted, "a great-aunt's plan
to visit from a distant state"); and requests by couples to change the marriage
vows or to refer to God by any other than His familiar name. Such requests
should be clearly and firmly declined, the Commission warned, and so should
petitions to substitute for church-approved hymns such popular musical favorites as Mendelssohn's "Wedding March" from *A Midsummer Night's Dream*
and Wagner's "Bridal Chorus" from *Lohengrin*. "Neither of these pieces is,
properly considered, sacred music," the report noted dryly. "They are drawn
from operatic contexts which are neither appropriate nor encouraging. The
Mendelssohn piece occurs at the 'wedding' of an ox to an ass, and the Wagner
piece precedes the tragic death of the bride who has been unfaithful to her
husband."

It is easy to be amused by the image such a document presents—of Waspy clerics in white collars sniffing down their noses at their congregants' lack of graces—but the picture is more complex than that. The clergy may abhor the excesses of Bridezilla culture—"I hate being a religious decoration at the narcissistic cleavage conventions we call weddings," Jody Vickery, a minister at Campus Church of Christ in Norcross, Georgia, wrote in *Christianity Today*—and even among very religious groups in America there seems to exist a sense that weddings are out of control: To combat the proliferation of ice sculptures and meat-carving stations at Orthodox Jewish celebrations, some rabbis have signed a pledge only to officiate at so-called guidelines weddings, at which limits—no more than eighteen hundred dollars on flowers; no more than four hundred guests, rather than the thousand guests who can sometimes attend an Orthodox wedding—have been instituted in an effort to spare the pockets of middle-class families who may well have half a dozen daughters to marry off within a short space of years.

But it hardly seems fair to disparage the bride (who, in Jody Vickery's choice turn of phrase, "is a bundle of nerves, sweats off her makeup and frets about her gown, which is always a size and a half too small") for seeking to follow the advice of bridal magazines to use her wedding as a vehicle for self-expression. It seems particularly unfair when some ministers are more than willing to permit such a use of their services—and especially when those ministers include Vickery himself, who once performed a cowboy-themed wedding ceremony, with saddles and bales of hay decorating the church, and a groom in chaps and a ten-gallon hat. For churches, no less than for the department stores with their bridal registries, weddings present an opportunity—for spreading the word of God, and, on a less elevated plane, for filling the pews of the church itself.

Like the Disney company, churches have recognized that being involved in the formation of families is a good way of encouraging those families to become repeat visitors. Some churches stage special "marriage and family" services, at which couples who have married in the church are invited back to renew their vows (and, perhaps just as alluring to many brides, are offered a repeat opportunity to wear their wedding gowns). Other churches advertise in the Wedding Facilities section of the Yellow Pages with the express purpose of attracting more souls to the congregation. "Our ads are very successful in bringing new people to us," the representative of one church in Palm Springs, California, told *Christianity Today*, estimating that 95 percent of couples who wed at his church were Yellow Pages referrals. Still others have decided that, if couples expect to treat their spiritual space as if it were a country club or a catering hall, the religious institution might as well reap some of the material benefits, too. The complaints of princess weddings delivered by Douglas G. Scott, the Radnor rector, in *Christianity Today* are somewhat undermined by the fact—unmentioned in his article—that his church happens to own a colonial farmhouse called Bolingbroke Mansion, also in Radnor, which has magnificent gardens and handsome function rooms, and is, according to the mansion's Web site, "the perfect setting for your perfect day."

And while there are clergy who are infuriated by requests on the part of marrying couples to write their own vows, or otherwise customize the standard wedding ceremony, many others encourage it as a means to make a wedding ceremony more meaningful to its participants. Some clergy have sought to establish new rituals to accommodate the peculiar dynamics of the contemporary wedding: One minister from Kansas City, Roger Coleman, markets through the Beverly Clark catalog a product called a Family Medallion—a pendant aimed at the remarriage market, featuring a symbol of three interlocking circles, available in all kinds of finishes ranging from silver-over-pewter to fourteen-karat gold inset with a diamond. The medallion, of which Coleman says he sells about ten thousand a year, is designed to be given after the exchange of wedding rings to any offspring one or both spouses may be bringing to their new union. (Coleman also sells Family

Medallion pins, rings, and charm bracelets for children whose tastes do not run to pendants.) The accommodation of the church to the expectation on the part of marrying couples that it offer them a wedding that is distinct in some way from the conventional standard may disturb some clerical authorities, but options marketing—in Joyce Gioia's phrase—seems to have found a place within religious institutions, too.

The concept of options marketing is a useful one for thinking about the entire sphere of organized religion in the United States. A suggestive line of thinking among sociologists who study religious practices in the United States proposes that the persistent religiosity of Americans—compared, say, to Northern Europeans, with whom they otherwise have much in common culturally—can be explained by the fact that without an established state faith, religious institutions in America are obliged to compete with one another. They do this by responding to the needs, demands, and tastes of potential congregants, rather than by assuming congregants will conform to the expectations of a clerical hierarchy: by offering specialized prayer groups, or child-care facilities, or bookstores, or teen-oriented rock concerts, and the like.

Religious institutions are similarly obliged to adapt to the demands of the wedding marketplace, since couples getting married have the option not only of taking their custom to another, more accommodating church, but may take their custom out of the church altogether to a catering hall or a country club, or even to a wedding chapel that offers the visual cues of churchiness—pews, stained-glass windows—without any of a church's more stringent demands, such as attendance at premarital counseling sessions. Churches want congregants, and weddings are one way to get them, even when that means making accommodations some clergy might prefer to avoid, such as importing bales of hay into the nave.

The problem with doing this is that the very accommodation of the religious institution to the wishes of the couple can easily undermine the reverence a religious institution is supposed to inspire. "I hate weddings," wrote Jody Vickery, the disgruntled minister from Georgia, in his *Christianity Today* article. "Funerals? I love them. At funerals people are shell-shocked by the ultimate realities of life, death, grief, and God." At funerals, Vickery was implying, churches still provided the institutional anchor—the institutional comfort—that a church wedding should also provide, but too often doesn't. He blamed the bride and groom for trivializing weddings. But the problem is not simply that today's couples have expectations of what a church might do for them in the way of a wedding that churches cannot accommodate; it is also that churches very often do accommodate those expectations, but do so ambivalently and with regret over the eclipse of the authority to which they feel entitled. And so while Joyce Gioia's couples might willingly embrace a ritual that had no institutional grounding, Vickery's couples, who came to the church with the expectation of an institutional grounding, might end up finding less of one than they had hoped for.

What does a church that is prepared to cede its authority over a religious ritual as important as a wedding offer to the bride and groom who are married therein? What need does such a church fulfill, if it is not the traditional need fulfilled by churches—of being a place to be baptized in, to worship in, to be married in, to find community in, to find succor in, to be buried by? In an attempt to answer this question, I went to the tiny township of Hebron, Wisconsin, one bright, cold weekend in early spring to visit Hebron Church, which is also known, for marketing purposes, as the Chapel on the Hill.

Hebron is a speck on the map halfway between Madison and Milwaukee and less than an hour from each. It has a population of about 250, just two roads, and no shops unless you count Kidd's truck dealership on the very edge of town. The only public institutions in Hebron are the Town Hall Museum, which is shuttered for all but three or four days per year; Pete's Place, a bar that is equipped with a television, a pool table, and montages of beer-company promotional posters showing friendly young women in shorts and tank tops; and the United Methodist church, which sits atop a rise overlooking the drowsy main street.

Hebron's first church was built in the 1850s, a couple of decades after the township was settled by farmers and manufacturers who had immigrated from Germany and Britain, as well as from states farther east. It stood for forty-odd years until its tower was struck by lightning one Sunday morning not long after services were completed, and the church imploded. Undaunted by this alarming act of God, the congregation rebuilt, and the structure that stands today, with its pressed-tin ceiling, curved wooden pews, white-painted exterior with gingerbread decoration, and stately Victorian stained-glass window overlooking the main street, was completed in the last year of the nineteenth century.

The view from the church door is one of immediate rural charm compromised by neglect. Many of the houses on the main street, which runs for about three-quarters of a mile down to a river, have been permitted to slide into ungraceful decline. There are porches furnished with bedraggled indoor furniture and overstocked with indistinct bits of machinery. Here and there exterior walls in need of repair have been plastered with Tyvek, while windows with inadequate glazing have been covered with dirtied transparent plastic sheeting, like elderly eyes misted over with cataracts. One splintered house at the low end of town, near the riverbank, seems some time ago to have buckled to its knees like a drunk, and having decided there was nothing much worth standing up for after that, simply stayed in that position. There used to be trees lining the street, forming a natural archway leading to the church, but they died from lack of care, and no one took the trouble to plant anew.

Hebron is the object of outsiders' interest so infrequently that an announcement of my impending arrival had appeared in the church newsletter the week before. I was met at Milwaukee Airport by Karen Klatt, the pastor of Hebron Church, who is a small, forceful woman with steel gray hair in a bowl cut and the avidity of a Girl Scout mistress tempered with a subversive liberal streak. Because Hebron has nothing approaching a hotel, I spent the night at Klatt's home in Sussex, forty-five minutes from her church. There, she explained to me that life was leaching out of Hebron, and out of Jefferson County, in which it sits, as a whole. The independent farms that used to dominate the region have been swamped by conglomerates and sold off for residences; manufacturing industries are threatened by the cheaper labor markets available overseas and by the area's general economic malaise. The elementary school on the hill closed down a generation ago, and the population is growing older, as young people born in the region discover that job opportunities are limited and tenuous and find themselves obliged to move elsewhere. The decline of Hebron has taken its toll on the church, too; while it has remained open, unlike many small churches in rural America, it has only thirty-odd members. "On an average Sunday, we get fifteen or twenty people," Klatt said. "And they are mostly World War Two veterans."

The church can only support a part-time pastor, a post that Klatt has held since 2000. Until her arrival the church made do with seminary students, who were assigned for two-year stints before moving on to a more thriving congregation; but when Klatt, who came to the ministry later in life, after raising a family, was drawing to the end of her time as a student there, she decided she wanted to stay on, and began to wonder whether the church might not have untapped resources with which her part-time salary might be supported and the congregation and community revived. Inspiration struck in the spring of 2002, and if its effects were less immediately cataclysmic than those of the bolt of lightning visited upon Hebron a century and a half earlier, it did, all the same, have the potential of shaking the church to its foundations. A longtime congregant who owned a dairy farm and had been widowed some years earlier was about to be remarried at Hebron Church, and during the preparations the bride happened to mention that her sister had been married in the Little Brown Church in Nashua, Iowa, which, in addition to performing the usual community functions, operates as a commercial wedding chapel, hosting more than four hundred ceremonies a year. Maybe, the bride suggested, Hebron Church should try the same thing.

This set Klatt—who, after graduating high school, had attended business school in nearby Whitewater—thinking. Perhaps some additional revenue could be made by opening the church outside of regular hours to couples wanting to make the ultimate commitment to each other within ecclesiastical walls, even if they didn't actually want to come to church the rest of the time. The chapel might even attract a few new members to the church, if an attachment to the site of their wedding were to draw them back for spiritual sustenance of a more consistent nature.

The decision to open the church up for weddings was not unanimously supported by its members. One woman, Deb Kutz, a lay leader of the congregation before Klatt's arrival, resigned in protest over the change. "People have said they don't want it to be Las Vegas, but I feel it is going that way," Kutz told me when I spoke with her about the chapel. "It's traditional, but it doesn't have the meaning of Jesus."

But Klatt saw no alternative. "I would love to tell you that it was a great spiritual experience," she said to me. "But it was a way to live out what the congregation saw as their mission, and to make money. And if that sounds too calculating—well, my first degree was in business, and I understand the language of marketing."

My visit to Hebron, about a year after Klatt's wedding-chapel experiment had begun, fell on the weekend before Easter. The Palm Sunday congregation was larger than usual, with about forty-five worshippers drawn by the service, and also drawn by the promise of the potluck brunch that was to take place in the church's basement afterward.

The church that morning was bright and sunny, and it felt full of life. A gaggle of towheaded members of the Sunday school, children with last names like Telfer and Foerster and Folker and Kahn, walked down the aisle waving palm fronds. The congregation sang the hymn "Rejoice, the Lord Is King," and the church organist, the wife of a minister from a neighboring congregation, pressed her keys while warbling above the general throng like an eighteenth-century castrato. When it came time for Pastor Karen to deliver her homily, she bounced on the balls of her feet by the altar and addressed the assembled with the peppy urgency of a sports-team coach. "Today we have a human God who was so glad to be with us that he rode on a donkey into Jerusalem," she said in her earnest, eager way. "This is the day to feel that Christians are winners, and not sinners. This is not the day to be bedraggled. Let us not be afraid to shout Hosanna and worship a king."

After the service I met Connie Polzin, the Chapel on the Hill's pro bono wedding planner, who was cutting up slices of coffee cake and serving pancakes in the kitchen, chatting with neighbors she'd known all her life. Polzin, a warm, guileless woman who works as a night janitor in nearby Fort Atkinson, was born and raised in Hebron—she calls herself "one of the baptism until burial people" —and joked that she had a certain expertise when it came to weddings at Hebron Church, having had two of them there herself (the first time, pregnant, at sixteen; the second time, wiser, ten years later).

It was Polzin who coordinated the weddings, of which there had been nine in the chapel's first year of operation, as well as one vow-renewal ceremony. Polzin distributed a brochure at local bridal fairs—"Have the wedding of your dreams in a charming country church," it read—and a promotional video had been made that showed a bride gazing mistily through the church's stained-glass windows. Polzin had begun to recruit other Hebronites to the wedding enterprise: a baker from a neighboring town made cakes for Chapel on the Hill couples; the regular church organist played the organ for one hundred dollars a ceremony, with a soprano solo costing fifty dollars extra. (Polzin's hopes of persuading the farmer who lives next door to the church to offer postceremonial horse-and-buggy rides had, she told me, so far come to naught.) Polzin had planted floral borders in front of the church to enhance wedding portraits shot there, and had dreams of a gazebo in the rear of the church, for summer weddings and photographic opportunities.

The second season at the chapel was shaping up to be even busier than the first, with calls coming in from couples who'd attended the weddings of friends or relatives there and wanted something similar for themselves. The point about the Chapel on the Hill, Polzin said, is that all comers are welcome, including those who've never attended church in their lives, or who have cohabited or had children before marriage—the kind of behaviors that might get them turned away from a regular church. "We'll do anything except Satanism," she told me, cheerfully.

A wedding was scheduled for the next day, Monday morning. "I've had to restrict my no-Lenten-weddings rule to Maundy Thursday and Easter Weekend," Klatt said, as we arrived at the church that day in advance of the couple, who had requested a small, simple wedding to coincide with their anniversary. (Just what it was the anniversary of, Klatt had not dared to ask.)

Connie Polzin was already there, fixing decorative bows to the ends of the pews, and not long afterward the bride, groom, and their two witnesses arrived at the same time, and huddled in the vestibule self-consciously, like guests just arriving at a costume party before they've had their first, inhibition-loosening cocktails. The bride had short blond hair, which had been swept up in a bobby-pinned crest, and she wore a huge shiny gown that bagged a little around the bodice and had lace sleeves, a basque waist, a huge bow at the base of the spine, and a train that looked to be about five feet long.

The groom wore black denim jeans, a white shirt, and a skinny black tie. "Are you going to walk down the aisle?" Klatt asked the bride, who demurred until her witness, dressed in a green bridesmaid's gown left over from another wedding, told her she had to. Klatt led the groom to the altar while the bride walked alone to the front of the church and, with a slightly abashed smile, fluffed out her own train and led herself briskly up the aisle. There was no music, and the only guests were a reporter from the local newspaper and myself.

I'd spoken to the bride a couple of weeks earlier to ask if I might sit in on her wedding, and she had explained that getting married in the Chapel on the Hill was a compromise between herself and her husband-to-be. He would have preferred a civil marriage, but she wanted at least a little ceremony, although it was important for them both to keep costs at a minimum. She'd bought the gown on sale a year or so earlier in the expectation that they would eventually get married, and she didn't intend to miss out on the opportunity of wearing it. She knew about the Chapel on the Hill because a friend had been married there, and so when she suggested it to her boyfriend he agreed, on the condition that they could do it very quietly, without their families present. Having been raised as a Methodist even though she was no longer a churchgoer, the bride also hoped that the Chapel on the Hill would provide her with enough of a sense of sanctity while not offending the sensibilities of her husband-to-be. "I don't want it to be real religious, and I don't want it to be the ten-minute courthouse deal," she told me.

The ceremony was neither. Klatt attempted to speak to the couple intimately about their lives, in spite of her short acquaintance with them, and she emphasized the spiritual nature of their commitment. "You are taking a very big step, and I am very, very glad that you have chosen to do it in a church," she said. "What you are doing is making a whole new family, and that is a good thing. We love both of you, and bless your marriage. This is a wonderful anniversary for you, even if you are not sure if it's eleven or twelve years."

There had been some discussion of the anniversary question in the vestibule before the ceremony—each remembered a different year of the start of their relationship—and there had also been some other rather surprising information disclosed. After the wedding was over, the couple told Klatt, they would be going to a wake; the bride's step-grandmother had died a few days earlier, and her funeral had been scheduled for exactly the same time as the wedding. Rather than canceling their plans, they had decided to go ahead and get married, then go straight to the wake. Their presence as newlyweds would be a big surprise, since not only had their families not been invited to the wedding, they mostly hadn't been told about it in the first place.

When the couple presented the news of the funeral to Klatt, moments before she was about to perform the wedding, her eyes widened, but she retained her composure; and during the ceremony she made graceful reference to the extraordinary circumstances. "After this ceremony you are going to a meal after a funeral," she said. "I am sorry you have to go to a party that is not in your honor, but you will be able to present yourself as life going on. I encourage you to share your news with your family. They will be astounded."

What had the Chapel on the Hill given this couple? After the wedding was over, the bride seemed delighted—if she wasn't exactly punching the air as Joyce Gioia's bride had done, she wasn't far off. The groom—who may have wondered how, having managed to keep his family away from the wedding, he had ended up with two reporters there—looked as if he were trying to pretend nothing much had happened, with a modest smile betraying his acknowledgment that, actually, no small thing had come to pass. But although Karen Klatt urged them to return to the church for a Sunday service, they didn't seem likely to do so. They had had their picturesque wedding in a charming country church, as the chapel's brochure had promised, and they had the pictures to prove it. When the ceremony was over, Connie Polzin had photographed the bride looking wistful by the stained-glass window; the couple on the steps to the altar, the marriage license poking out of the groom's breast pocket like a handkerchief; and a shot of their newly beringed hands clasping. "He's going to take the ring off as soon as we get outside," the bride had said, with a big smile, and Polzin asked if he worked somewhere he couldn't wear a ring. "He don't work. He was laid off," said the groom's best man, his brother, at which the groom shrugged.

What they hadn't experienced was the kind of wedding Connie Polzin underwent both times she had been married in Hebron Church—one in which the church provided not only a charming setting but a familiar community. Of course, neither of Polzin's weddings conformed to the standards that might be expected of a traditional church wedding, given that she was pregnant the first time and had been divorced the second; but both were church weddings in the sense that Polzin belonged to the church, and the church belonged to Polzin.

Karen Klatt was more than aware of what was lacking in Chapel on the Hill weddings—she told me that she cringed when prospective couples would remark upon the photo opportunities the church presented—but she seemed hopeful that couples like this one nonetheless drew something spiritual from the experience. "A lot of the people we marry have no idea what churches do," she said. "But they must have some yearning for the divine, otherwise they wouldn't want to be married in a church."

Whether the wish on the part of this couple and the others who married in Klatt's church amounted to a yearning for the divine, or merely a yearning for the picturesque, as Deb Kutz, the church member who resigned over the chapel had feared, was impossible to tell. But if Joyce Gioia's wedding ceremony had struck me, in the end, as being like a dip into a shallow pool of mixed, muddied waters, this one felt hollowed out, like the empty shell of a nut from which most of the wholesome meat has been scooped.

The hollowness seemed to belong not just to this wedding in particular, but to the entire wedding chapel enterprise in Hebron. For Karen Klatt the chapel was a hedge against the prospect of decline: The only way to save the church, it seemed, was to sell the church, and to put to commercial use the attractive environs that were intended for anything but. Klatt had hardly turned Hebron Church into a Las Vegas–style wedding machine, as her detractors feared, but the Chapel on the Hill nonetheless traded on a sentimental idealization of the very thing that the Hebron Church could not on its own sustain: the endurance of a thriving community of souls. The only way that the church could fill its coffers was to market itself to couples who, in the usual course of events, declined to fill its pews.

The yearning of both Klatt's and Gioia's couples, I suspected, was neither for the divine, exactly, nor merely for the picturesque, but rather for a sense of propriety: for the sanction of some authority larger than themselves—be that Gioia, with her free-form spirituality, or Karen Klatt, with her pragmatic bow to commerce. Both couples, in different ways, had found themselves without a wedding script to follow, and had been obliged to improvise a new one the best they could: in the case of Gioia's couple, by reaching beyond their own traditions, and in the case of Klatt's, by gathering up a few scraps from their own.

Perhaps this amounted to the "spin on tradition" of which Antonia van der Meer had spoken at the Business of Brides conference, or the wedding ceremony as an expression of one's personal sense of style, as Colin Cowie had proposed; but in each case it seemed to me that by jettisoning the old structures, and the old orders, both couples had been left with a wedding ceremony that was significantly lighter in weight than it deserved to be. Meanwhile, the finality of the funeral to which Klatt's couple was departing— I watched them head off to their car, the bride carrying a camera bag in one hand and her train in the other—served, just as the promise of the pregnancy of Gioia's bride had done, as a reminder of every wedding day's irresistible, irrefutable gravity.

Seven

Love Me Tender

Karen Klatt had not turned the township of Hebron into a wedding factory, for good or for ill; but what of those places in America for which the wedding business does constitute an important part of the economy? Klatt told me that shortly after she had come up with the idea of the Chapel on the Hill she happened to have taken a vacation in Gatlinburg, Tennessee, the so-called Honeymoon Capital of the South. There, she said, the winding mountain roads were lined with commercial wedding chapels; and while she had no intention of decking her church with cupids or installing a romantic waterfall in a corner of the parking lot, she suggested that I go and see the place myself.

And so, not long after leaving Hebron, I went to Gatlinburg in the hope of finding out what a wedding-industry town has to offer the brides and grooms who go there to get married—about eighteen thousand of them each year, nearly five weddings for every year-round resident. Gatlinburg has a delightful natural setting: Located on the edge of the Great Smoky Mountains

National Park, it dwells along a river in a valley, green peaks rising on its two flanks. The mountainsides are largely unmarked by development, but for a lodge or a ski lift here or there, and within them lie hiking trails that lead visitors deep into temperate, emerald forest. Gatlinburg itself, by contrast, is a bustle of commerce. Rustic lodges line the main street, advertising their in-room fireplaces and their Jacuzzi-equipped bathrooms. Tourists in loungewear and sneakers occupy the lodges' second-story decks at cocktail hour, watching the scene below like birds with primary-color plumage and big white claws perched on telegraph wires.

Like Dollywood, the theme park in the stylized form of an old mountain town that Dolly Parton built in her hometown of Pigeon Forge a few miles away—it features a street of quaint wooden houses climbing up a hillside and a replica of the two-room shack that was Parton's childhood home, equipped with one iron bedstead to serve a family of twelve—Gatlinburg has transformed its hardscrabble history into an entertainment experience for today's tourist. There is Hillbilly Golf, a miniature-golf course set into the challengingly steep hillside, and a dense shopping district with stores named Hillbilly Heaven and Things Unique and The Fudgery and The Kandy Kitchen, none of which sell much other than sweets, T-shirts, and souvenir teddy bears. The atmosphere is one of commercialized down-homeyness: Auntie Anne's pretzel store is directly across the street from Aunt Mahalia's Candies, and I counted three different galleries selling the paintings of Thomas Kinkade, the master of mass-produced small-town sentimentalia. There is diversion for the sensation-seeking: A Ripley's Believe It or Not is on one street corner, and a few steps away, a virtual-reality ride that simulates the experience of being on a catastrophic railway journey during an earthquake. Gatlinburg is in the Bible Belt, and some of its diversions are explicitly aimed at the Christian tourist market. At Christus Gardens visitors can view a series of dioramas depicting the life of Jesus, and on the main street, Christian-themed emporia sell hipster T-shirts printed with slogans such as ARMY OF THE LORD: SERVING GOD IS NOT JUST A JOB, IT'S AN ADVENTURE, and baby bibs decorated with the words ITTY BITTY BAPTIST or MIGHTY LIL METHODIST.

Gatlinburg's wedding-chapel industry, like the rest of the town to which it belongs, offers prepackaged quaintness with a distinctly Christian flavor— and, crucially, a relatively low cost. The priciest wedding packages in town, such as a ceremony and buffet reception for fifty guests at the Chapel in the Glen, a wooden churchlike structure built in the forested hills on the outskirts of town, costs only about $3,800. A basic package at a chapel can be had for under $200. There are innumerable different places to get married in Gatlinburg: about twenty independent chapels, as well as the in-room or on-site gazebo weddings offered by many lodges. Couples can choose Cupid's Chapel of Love, where plastic ground cover has been planted in the flower beds edging the parking lot and a sign reading DO NOT DISTURB: CUPID AT WORK is placed at the doorway when a wedding is in progress; or can draw upon the town's hillbilly heritage by opting to be married by Dan Rhymer, a former taxidermist for the Smithsonian Institution with a gray beard as bushy as any taxidermy specimen, who performs ceremonies at his mountainside home or at a couple's rental cabin while wearing a denim bib, black frock coat, and big black hat. Weddings are also performed at the Garters & Guns Old Tyme Saloon, a photography studio in a storefront on Gatlinburg's main street that resembles a stage set of a bawdy saloon, in which tourists sit for sepia-toned portraits while sporting a Stetson or squeezing into a corset modeled on Victorian bordello fashions. The dedicated wedding chapel— should the saloon environs not appeal—consists of a back room decorated with trompe l'oeil woodland scenes, for those priced out of an actual woodland wedding.

The first wedding chapel in Gatlinburg opened in 1979, and its founder, a Baptist minister called Reverend Charles Edwin Taylor who goes by Rev Ed, is still a dominant figure in the town's wedding business—which, I discovered when I started talking to chapel owners, is as competitive and as riven with rivalry as any other commercial enterprise. Rev Ed is a controversial figure in Gatlinburg, having washed up in town in the late seventies with a past that, by his own admission, was soiled by secular transgressions, including divorce and a history of alcohol abuse. The conduct of his business has not been flaw-less, either: His organization, Gatlinburg Ministries, Inc., has been repeat-edly sued by the Department of Labor for violations of fair labor laws, most recently in 2000. Taylor claimed to have done nothing wrong, but agreed to pay about $120,000 in civil penalties, and in back wages and damages, to forty former employees. "Satan is trying to put a crimp in the cause of Christ," Tay-lor told the local newspapers at the time of the investigation.

The day after I arrived in town, I visited Taylor, who claims to have per-sonally married more than forty thousand couples, at his complex of small wedding chapels that lies upon a downtown side street. Taylor, who is in his seventies, appeared very fit—he told me he runs two miles, six days a week—and had gleaming teeth. He wore a clergyman's collar and a pendant bearing a silver coin, which he insisted I take a good look at. "That was stamped and minted fifty years before Christ was born," he said. "It is called the Shekel of Tyre. For thirty pieces of this coin right here, Judas betrayed the Lord."

His motivation for entering the wedding business, he told me, was religious rather than commercial. "Everyone that comes here gets a Bible, autographed by me with the date of their marriage," he said. "They get an au-diotape of their ceremony that lasts fifteen to twenty minutes, and it is done right, with the sanctity of God's blessings upon it. Now, if you walk into one of these other chapels, the minister has been told by the owner that he only has two to three minutes to perform the ceremony. What can you say in two to three minutes, relative to laying the groundwork and principle for a Christian marriage?" Such questions are, apparently, waived whenever Valentine's Day falls on a weekend, when Taylor holds a round-the-clock "Marry-thon" in a so-far unsuccessful attempt to establish a world record.

Taylor explained that even before he arrived in Gatlinburg the town had long been a place in which it was easy to obtain a quick marriage ceremony. "They were being married by a JP out in a little country store where he stood with tobacco juice dribbling off his chin," he said. "I thought, wait a minute, these folks deserve to be married with dignity, sanctity, and credibility, and have God's blessing upon their lives." He started with one small wooden chapel, eventually adding more buildings to create what he referred to as a village, but which looked to me more like a ramshackle collection of buildings squeezed into every corner of the lot's available space. Couples today can choose to participate in the ongoing construction themselves: They may buy a brick bearing their names to be set into the sidewalk to commemorate their wedding day in pedestrian perpetuity.

Taylor's downtown location is convenient—his chapels are only steps from the government marriage license bureau—but it lacks the woodland seclusion enjoyed by some of its rival chapels. For years, Taylor has adopted aggressive tactics in the face of all competition, and in the late 1990s he waged a campaign to alter the state's marriage legislation so that it would prohibit ministers who had acquired their credentials from the Universal Life Church or other Internet or mail-order interests from being able to conduct weddings in Tennessee. (As part of his effort to discredit online credentials, lodged an application for his dog to become a Universal Life minister. He displayed the certificate on his Web site.) "Oh, there are some pretty chapels out there, but it is like Jesus said, they may appear to be beautiful on the outside, but on the inside they are like raving wolves and full of dead men's bones," Taylor told me, loosely quoting Christ's castigation of the Pharisees.

Taylor's efforts to outlaw rival ministers have so far not succeeded, but it remains a pillar of his marketing strategy to suggest that weddings conducted at chapels other than his own may not be legal, a suggestion which has made him an extremely unpopular figure among the fraternity of chapel owners in Gatlinburg. "I think it is dangerous, spiritually dangerous to use the Lord and his Church in that manner—in order to gain business, and to use it as a tool for marketing," David Faulkner, the head of the Wedding Chapel Association of Gatlinburg and the owner of the Sugarland Wedding Chapel, told me when I visited him after spending time with Reverend Taylor. "I don't think God looks in favor upon that." Faulkner's objection struck me as more personal than theological: The Web site for his own chapel informs potential clients that "all of our wedding ceremonies are strictly religious" and adds, "Members of other religions that do not consider themselves Christian are welcome, but please do not ask our ministers to change the Christian nature of the ceremony or remove our religious symbols." Faulkner, who is a retired Baptist minister himself, hinted cryptically to me that he believed God might tire of Rev Ed's practices sufficiently to deliver an Old Testament–style smiting. "I have been involved in meetings in which this individual has said certain things, and I have gotten up and walked to the back of the room because I didn't want to be around if something happened," Faulkner said. "I don't think the Lord tolerates that stuff forever."

The lurid antagonisms between the chapel owners in Gatlinburg make for choice gothic entertainment. But to the brides and grooms who come to Gatlinburg to get married, none of that antagonism is apparent: Gatlinburg is just a cute little town with a lot of cute little chapels. The chapels offer a mountain-dwelling version of the traditionalesque, trading proudly upon the reputation of the region and its inhabitants as rural, isolated, and unsophisticated. In a way, Gatlinburg's wedding business is the antithesis of Bridezilla culture. What is being peddled in Gatlinburg is not nuptial excess, but nuptial simplicity: an unfussy ceremony conducted in a building that looks not like a church of the sort that a visitor to Gatlinburg might actually belong to—one with a modern facility, a huge parking lot, and a bookstore or a snack bar on the premises—but that looks like the popular idea of a rural church.

But the chapels in Gatlinburg offer more than just the quaint facsimile of a simple, rural church wedding. They offer a fantasy of a less complicated life than is to be had in the everyday world beyond Gatlinburg—the world in which stores sell groceries and cleaning supplies rather than candy, and in which houses are functionally built of concrete and drywall rather than from forest-hewn logs. Many of the couples who come to Gatlinburg to get married, David Faulkner explained to me, do so because these are second marriages, and the participants are uncomfortable with marrying in their home church in front of family and friends who have already seen them enact this supposedly once-and-forever ritual.

Thirty years ago, a second wedding was generally an occasion for modesty, with perhaps a civil ceremony for a few family members and a nicely tailored suit in a pastel color for the bride. Today's remarrying divorcée—in Gatlinburg and beyond—has a flattering new appellation, that of the "encore bride," which makes a second wedding sound like an occasion for a standing ovation. She shares all the perquisites of the first-time bride: She can wear a gown no less big and white than she did the first time, and she can command a party as grand and a guest list and registry list no shorter. In fact, she is at an advantage over the first-time bride, since she knows what didn't work about her first wedding—beyond the union with her first husband—and can rectify her mistakes. One wedding planner named Christine Figliuolo, from Waldwick, New Jersey, told me about a client who had wept through every planning session, called just weeks after the wedding and said that every moment of the honeymoon had been awful, and was divorced shortly thereafter. Nonetheless, Figliuolo said, the bride had told her, "Chris, when I plan my next wedding, I want to plan it with you."

The remarriage client base is an attractive one for the wedding industry, which will take all the brides it can get: As an article in *Vows* magazine asked its bridal-store-owning readers, "Are you reaching the future remarriage market by serving the current generation's brides well?" But the business of selling weddings within a culture in which divorce is so prevalent is ripe with paradox.

To each remarrying divorcée or divorcé there is likely to be a clear rationale for this particular second marriage; when it comes to marriage, older often does mean wiser. (Samuel Johnson famously called second marriage the triumph of hope over experience, but it can also be the triumph of experience over experience.) Marriages and weddings are very different things, even though the wedding industry tends to conflate them for marketing purposes, as JCPenney did with its wedding-picture-style advertisements that promised endurance both from true love and from cookware. But the failure rate of marriages, one would think, might make selling weddings a difficult proposition: If Ford's cars or Maytag's washing machines had the same record of success as do American marriages, both companies would be out of business. How is it that the wedding industry manages to persuade people— not just those who have been divorced themselves, but everyone who knows anyone who's been divorced—to keep buying?

One way—the way of Bridezilla culture, which insists that a wedding is an expression of individual taste and style—is to make the experience of planning a wedding and of being a bride so intoxicating that the daunting reality of married life to which it leads recedes in significance when compared with the more immediately pressing issues of choosing invitation typefaces or selecting bridesmaids' dresses. Wedding-planning euphoria is so widespread that The Knot has created an entire message board devoted to "Wedding Withdrawal," for newlyweds experiencing postnuptial letdown. ("It's been 6 months since my wedding and sometimes I think back more so about the not so positive things, like dress not fitting, the bad sunburn I got the day before the wedding. I think back in my mind how I would have changed things and made them better. I mean, for a year we spend time planning this one day event and then boom it's over and it's like back to reality.")

Gatlinburg offered an alternative to the imperatives of Bridezilla culture. "Just because people don't have a lot doesn't mean they shouldn't have something nice," the aspiring wedding planner from Brooklyn who staged a winter-wonderland wedding on a two-hundred-dollar budget had said at the Association of Bridal Consultants training seminar. Gatlinburg's couples could get something nice—a proper white wedding—even for two hundred dollars.

But they were getting more than a low-budget wedding. Rev Ed told me that he started the business because brides and grooms "deserve to be married with dignity, sanctity, and credibility," and he was not alone in sounding a rhetorical note that said a ceremonial wedding was a basic right. A few years before my visit to Gatlinburg, a change in the state's marriage law threatened to raise the cost of a marriage license from just shy of forty dollars to nearly one hundred dollars, with couples being exempt from the surcharge of sixty dollars if they were willing to undergo a four-hour marriage preparation class. The new law was the product of an effort by some lawmakers to address Tennessee's very high rate of divorce—the third highest in the nation in 2000, when the legislation was introduced—but in Gatlinburg, the proposal was greeted as a violation of a fundamental value. It was "messing in the most private and sacred thing before two people," according to Senator Bill Clabough, in whose district Gatlinburg falls.

The legislation was also, of course, threatening to mess with the economic interests of the senator's business community. But the senator's words were not merely an elevated cover for lowlier business concerns. In Gatlinburg, where the pioneering spirit of the region's settlers is commemorated in log cabin motor lodges and hillbilly golf courses, the freedom to have the wedding ceremony of one's choice—in a chapel decked with plastic flowers, or on a mountainside with a minister in a denim bib—is an expression of an idealized way of life. Gatlinburg provides for its encore brides and grooms a means to erase their inconvenient marital histories and to begin again—but to do so in a context that assures them of their own adherence to tradition and to traditional morality. And Gatlinburg offers all its visitors a sentimentalized rendering of its own history, in which the rude and meager subsistence of a mountain farming community is transformed into a community of log cabin holiday residences with drive-up parking and an ice-cream parlor or funnel-cake vendor on every street corner. The promise of a Gatlinburg wedding is that marriage itself will prove to be as sweet as a sugar-powdered funnel cake, and as warm as a winterized log cabin with Jacuzzi suite; and it will be so even in those cases when an earlier marriage has already proven to be otherwise.

Weddings—in Gatlinburg and beyond—rarely acknowledge or accommodate any sense that marriage vows might be provisional rather than absolute, which is no surprise: If they did, it would be that much harder to go through with them. But there is one place where the sense of marriage as a provisional engagement rather than an unbreakable commitment is omnipresent, albeit submerged beneath glitz and excitement: Las Vegas.

Everyone who gets married in Las Vegas—more than 122,000 couples a year, at the most recent count—must go first to the Clark County courthouse downtown to get a marriage license, and when I went to the city a few weeks after I'd been in Gatlinburg, the Clark County courthouse was where I headed.

The wedding chapels and other wedding venues of Las Vegas present outlandish diversions far beyond those on offer even in Gatlinburg: a drive-through wedding at the Little White Wedding Chapel's "Tunnel of Vows" (actually less a tunnel than a curving carport painted with a trompe l'oeil sky populated by cherubs); an ersatz Renaissance wedding conducted by an opera-singing gondolier in a striped jersey plying his way along the Venetian hotel's abbreviated Grand Canal—which, in a showy feat of engineering, has been installed one floor up from the rattling casino and, in a radical reconceiving of the architectural unities of the city to which the hotel pays homage, cuts plain through a corner of the Piazza San Marco.

At the Clark County courthouse, however, I found that the Las Vegas wedding industry was stripped of its show-business drag. The courthouse was an institutional gray-painted building set back from the street up some concrete steps. Marriage licenses were issued twenty-four hours a day from an office to the right of the lobby, while to the left was Clark County's traffic court, so that when the traffic court was in session speed-signal violators were obliged to shuffle their way through metal detectors only steps from couples filling out their application forms, as if marriage itself were a form of petty criminality. (Since my visit to Las Vegas, a new courthouse has opened which has, mercifully enough, a separate entrance for those seeking to acquire a marriage license rather than pay a traffic-violations fine; and the marriage bureau's hours are now limited to 8 a.m. to midnight.)

It was early evening, but the temperature was still about one hundred degrees. A half dozen men and women were loitering on the scorched sidewalk and handing out flyers, all of them looking sun-dazed and punchy. These were the so-called hand-billers, hired by some of the city's chapels to perform last-minute marketing as couples arrived to get their licenses. As I made my own approach to the courthouse, one of the hand-billers, a tall young man in a red T-shirt and flip-flops who had the deep red-tanned skin of a beach bum or a vagrant, approached with a flyer in his hand. "Are you looking for a chapel?" he said, falling in step with me.

When I explained my reason for being there, he was eager to explain his own. His name was Randall, and he worked for a chapel called the Garden of Love. "We try to make everyone's day special, but it's a numbers game—get them in, get them out, boom, boom, boom," he said. (I'd stopped by the Garden of Love myself earlier in the day and had seen what he meant: In the lobby there were brides and grooms in their wedding finery, either on their way to be married or completing the paperwork afterward, while the owner, a young woman in a shabby T-shirt and shorts that exposed a tattooed thigh, dashed among them, and, oddly enough, a small monkey that was tethered by a leash to a cage hopped around furiously.) Randall had a background in sales: "I sold Nabisco cookies, golf clubs, educational software—if there's a sales position, I've been in it," he told me. Recently he'd been working for a tele- phone service company, cold-calling potential customers and trying to get them to switch plans. "I told them I had a better *program*, but I didn't tell them I had a better *price*," he explained slyly.

The hand-billers' window of opportunity to make a connection with a po- tential client was tiny, Randall explained: They were forbidden by law from distributing flyers on the courthouse steps, which were county property rather than city property, so they had to deliver their sales pitch in the few moments after the prospective client had exited the taxicab but was still on the sidewalk. "They are in Vegas, and they know that everyone is trying to get a buck from them, so they go to the first person that made contact with them," Randall said. "I try to help them out, tell them where to go for the license." A couple walked up and Randall stepped close, giving them a big smile.

"Are you here for a marriage license? Do you have your chapel already?" he asked.

"We're going to the Silver Bells," the man said.

"Congratulations, you guys," Randall said, and turned away, not wasting time on a lost cause. (Other passersby who were transparently off-limits were ignored, too. A very young woman in a pink sweat suit walked by hand- in-hand with an awkward-looking middle-aged man who wore a pocket pro- tector tucked into his short-sleeved shirt. "Prostitute," said one of the hand-billers, keeping his flyers to himself.)

The atmosphere on the sidewalk was warily collegial, with hand-billers from rival chapels trash-talking one another for my benefit, but without true conviction. But not long before I visited Las Vegas the competition between chapels had erupted into what the *Las Vegas Weekly* referred to as "The Chapel Wars." A wedding chapel owner named Cliff Evarts, whose Las Vegas Wedding Bureau was only steps from the courthouse, alleged that Cheryl Luell, the tattooed owner of the Garden of Love, had, along with her husband and an employee, adopted threatening and intimidating tactics on the sidewalk. (As the *Las Vegas Review-Journal* reported, one Wedding Bureau employee signed an affidavit stating that he had overheard someone associated with the Garden of Love say that he would beat Evarts "until he was dead.") Luell denied the charges, maintaining that her competitors were jealous of her professional success. (Perhaps predictably, her chapel shortly thereafter became the location for a reality television show.) A police task force was created to investigate reports of unruly and illegal behavior outside the courthouse, which included hand-billers being paint-balled, car tires being slashed, and homeless men being hired to beat up rival chapel employees. Sherrie Klute, the owner of the Stained Glass Wedding Chapel and Crystal Cathedral, told a reporter that she had hired armed guards to accompany her when she went to the courthouse. "We are the wedding capital of the world, and we've got a war zone out there," she said.

The courthouse wasn't a war zone when I visited, but it was one of the most insalubrious places in which I have ever spent time, and not just because of the men and women with their flyers on the sidewalk jostling to reach their potential clients. Inside the courthouse, where a sign on the wall warned against the bearing of firearms, the pace of arrivals picked up as day moved into evening, and the lobby became fraught with an air of agitation, as disconcerting as a metallic taste in the mouth. Couples arrived two by two after a day by the pool or at the roulette tables, flushed from excitement and perhaps also from the effects of cocktail hour, though licenses are not supposed to be issued to anyone who is clearly inebriated. The parade of humanity passing through was as colorful and, on occasion, as theatrically degraded as if the scene had been cast by Fellini. A group of four who were planning a double wedding arrived and began to fill out their application forms. One of the women wore a headband with devil's horns attached, while the other had on a T-shirt printed with the words DIRTY WHITE SLUT. The groom of the Dirty White Slut, a double amputee, was in a wheelchair. The horned bride's groom read the questions on the application aloud, and when he got to the question that asked how many times he had been married before, he cried out, "This is number four! Ding, ding, ding! I get the high score of the day!" and made a noise like a slot machine making a very satisfying payout.

I struck up a conversation with an affable security guard who was sitting in a booth near the courthouse entrance, with a disposable camera close at hand in case a celebrity bride or groom showed up. A few months earlier Britney Spears had arrived in the courthouse in the predawn hours to acquire a license to marry her childhood friend Jason Alexander at the Little White Wedding Chapel, and the security guard showed me a flyer relating to that marriage that he said had recently been in circulation. (The union was annulled after two days on the legal grounds that Spears "lacked understanding of her actions to the extent that she was incapable of agreeing to the marriage.")

"Beware of sollicitors or people passing out flyers about their wedding chapels in front of the marriage license bureau," the flyer read, with the spelling and punctuation of a ransom note. "They are very forceful and will try to distract you by saying unkind things about other wedding chapels. . . . They will use the tactics that Britany Spears was married in their chapel (which is false advertizing) and will even show you pictures of her. The Little White Wedding Chapel is famous all over the world and Britany Spears plus many other famous stars have been married in this chapel."

It struck me as odd that a wedding chapel would use the swiftly annulled nuptials of a wayward starlet as a marketing tool to attract couples who, presumably, intended to be married for more than two days. But in Vegas, who knew? Perhaps the bride in the DIRTY WHITE SLUT T-shirt would like nothing better than to follow in the nuptial footsteps of Spears. Certainly it was a possibility. While there is in Las Vegas more than enough of the hearts-and-flowers sentimentality that tends to characterize the wedding chapels in Gatlinburg—the Little White Wedding Chapel itself has a floral gazebo tucked into the curve of its drive-through "Tunnel of Love," for those who prefer a stationary ceremony—there is also the sense that a wedding might consist of anything its participants would like it to, and that its governing spirit might be ironic rather than sentimental.

In 1967, Joan Didion wrote about the Las Vegas wedding industry in her essay "Marrying Absurd," in which she observed the wishing wells and stained-glass paper windows of the chapels on the strip, the drunken bride in the orange minidress stumbling from altar to Cadillac Coupe de Ville, and the pregnant bride too young for the pink champagne served in her honor. The Las Vegas wedding industry, Didion concluded, was "merchandising 'niceness,' the facsimile of proper ritual, to children who do not know how else to find it, how to make the arrangements, how to do it 'right.'"

There is still some of that kind of absurdity to be had in Las Vegas, but what is marketed in Las Vegas today is not the ritual propriety sought by Didion's brides, but rather the specific and improper flavor of a Las Vegas wedding, with all its stylized tawdriness and its atmosphere of the ill-considered and illicit. Although it is still the place to go for a quickie wedding, Las Vegas doesn't play the same role that it did in the 1960s; rather, it's become the place to go to enact the idea of a quickie wedding. Tackiness and absence of gravity aren't accidental by-products of the Las Vegas wedding industry; they are its main selling point, accreted over generations of nuptial scurrility.

This is certainly the modus operandi at the Viva Las Vegas chapel, where the catalog of themed ceremonies available includes a gangster wedding with a Godfather as officiant; a James Bond wedding featuring dancing Bond girls and a ceremony performed by 007, who enters the chapel in a sports car; and a Gothic wedding, officiated by either Count Dracula or the Grim Reaper, who emerges from a coffin to seal the couple's vows. The Viva Las Vegas chapel offers the following proposition: that if a wedding ceremony does not have the meaning that most of the time we unthinkingly expect of it—if it does not initiate a couple's intimacy, if it does not amount to a transition to maturity, if it does not indicate an intention to start a family, if it does not require the sanction of a religious authority, if it need not be witnessed by the couple's community, and if it does not necessarily commit them to a life-long union—then it might as well be a lark as anything else.

One evening at the Viva Las Vegas chapel I observed the wedding of a couple, tourists from England, who told me that when they had finally decided it was time to marry—they had been together for years, and already had children—they had determined to combine a cermony with a vacation with family and friends. This was not a spur-of-the-moment event but one upon which a lot of planning had clearly been lavished. The groom and his three groomsmen were all wearing shiny white plastic Elvis jumpsuits, open to the waist, big medallions, and black wigs with heavy sideburns. The groom wore a distinguishing white plastic cape as well. The bridesmaids wore white go-go boots and minidresses in a black-and-white geometric pattern, and everyone looked very excited and happy. As the father of the bride, who also wore an Elvis suit and wig, led his daughter, who wore a white minidress and a veil, down the aisle of the high, vaulted chapel, Ron DeCar, the chapel's owner and an accomplished Elvis impersonator, who was in a white sequined jumpsuit of his own, sang "Can't Help Falling in Love with You." Throughout the ceremony, which lasted about twenty minutes, DeCar swiveled his hips, mumbled the vows in a mock-Tennessee drawl, and said "Thankyouvurrymuch" repeatedly. When he sang "Love Me Tender," he invited the bride and groom to dance, and they shuffled in circles together, the groom's cape and the bride's veil billowing gently behind them.

The whole thing was surprisingly affecting. The couple had entered the artificiality of the setup so completely as to transcend it; sincerity was generated out of the combustion of cheesiness and irony. Their wedding ceremony was, in some sense, superfluous: They already shared a home, had children, and were as deeply implicated with each other as was possible without a marriage certificate. There was no need for their wedding to be anything other than this touching and silly performance; and while it may not have emphasized the dignity and sanctity that Rev Ed had insisted he provided to his Gatlinburg couples, it had its own strange credibility. The tenderness was true.

Eight

Manufacturing Memories

The British tourists whose wedding ceremony the Elvis impersonator performed in Las Vegas (or rather, whose wedding ceremony the Elvis impersonator pretended to perform, since their official, legal ceremony was conducted by a minister with the requisite credentials in a side room immediately after the costumed festivities) were accompanied by only a few friends and family members. Their children, among other relations, had been left at home. But anyone—family, friends, or random strangers—could have viewed their ceremony via the webcam on the chapel's Web site, which broadcasts wedding visuals live around the clock. The couple could also have taken home a DVD of the ceremony, as well as an album of photographs, including those for which they posed in front of the chapel's digital street sign, where their names were broadcast to passing traffic. The event seemed unforgettable enough—it is not every day that one gets to see both one's husband and one's father wearing a wig and white jumpsuit—but the visual recording of the event was as essential an element of their wedding as was the hurriedly signed marriage certificate.

A live webcam wedding broadcast is still a novelty for which there is little demand, even in Las Vegas. But the creation of a visual record of the wedding day has been sought by brides and grooms for almost as long as the technology to do so has existed. "The wedding is one day, and then you have your memories; and the memories start to fade, and then you have your pictures," Susan Schneider, then the executive editor of *Modern Bride* magazine, had said at the Wedding March on Madison, informing her listeners that most wedding planners advise their brides never to cut corners on photography. If the bride pays attention to the urgings of the wedding industry, the obligation to secure an appropriately romantic, stylish, and emotionally resonant visual record of the day can come to loom as large, or even larger, than the management of the day itself. On the message boards of The Knot, there are contributions from brides who are spending more than a third of their total budget for the wedding on photography, which means, inevitably, cutting back in other areas. "We served chicken to make up for the photo splurge and I am so glad I did," wrote one.

Why is a wedding album such a priority? Why would a bride choose to scale back her expectations for the day itself—to serve chicken to her guests, rather than beef—so as to secure the anticipated pleasure of the day's private retrospection? In the hopes of beginning to answer questions such as these, I went one Saturday on assignment with Stefan and Linda Bright, a husband-and-wife team of wedding photographers who are based in Warren, New Jersey, and who work all over New Jersey and New York.

The Brights, whom I had met at a wedding-industry networking event, were unlikely participants in Bridezilla culture. They met in 1970 at an ashram in upstate New York, where they lived a frugal existence devoted to meditation and the renunciation of material things. Seven years later they renounced the ashram, and ran away to get married. (They did it at Windows on the World, the restaurant at the top of the World Trade Center, in a wedding whose adherence to prevailing bourgeois standards was designed to satisfy Stefan's mother.) When I met them they still carried with them the traces of their hippie past: Linda, who was gentle and kind, had a sadness about her, as if the world had been a harsher place than it promised to be when she was a flower child; while Stefan, whose gray hair fell in curling locks around his shoulders, had obscure symbols tattooed on his body, and— with very little encouragement—would explain his conviction that the earth had been subject to extraterrestrial visitations in the Sumerian period of history, at which time humankind had been subject to genetic modification by the alien visitors.

Like most successful wedding photographers working today, they specialized not just in portraiture but in so-called photojournalistic-style pictures—in which the photographer, instead of lining up family members and asking everyone to smile, maneuvers his or her way around the event, keeping an eye out for what one photographer on an online message board I came across referred to as "iconic moments." Such pictures may appear to the uninitiated to be more spontaneous than the formal poses used in traditional wedding photography, but it is not necessary to look at the portfolios of too many wedding photographers to discover that certain images are produced as routinely and reliably as the cake-cutting shot of old. Their aesthetic antecedent is not so much news photography as mass-market poster art. The shot of the bride's pale arms draped around the dark-suited shoulders of her groom, perhaps holding her bouquet and certainly displaying her engagement and wedding ring, is a favorite; and if the wedding party includes a flower girl, the wedding album can almost be guaranteed to include an image of her slumped in tiredness in a corner somewhere, her fairy-tale gown prettily mussed.

The project of the wedding photographer is not so much to represent reality as it is to offer an enhanced version of it: Susan Schneider, the *Modern Bride* editor who spoke about photography at the Wedding March on Madison, told a cautionary tale about a bride who complained that her wedding photographs made her arms look fat, which is another way of saying he failed to make her arms look thin. "I always say that a celebrity is a bride on the day of her wedding, and a bride is a celebrity on the day of her wedding," Sharon Sacks, the Los Angeles–based celebrity wedding planner who was a favorite of Jennifer Lopez, told me; and with this neat little formula, Sacks expressed the prevailing goal of all wedding photography: that the bride must be made to look as much like an image from a celebrity magazine as possible. With the widespread availability of procedures such as Botox or Restylane injections, and the popularity of cosmetic dentistry and over-the-counter teeth-whitening products, the polish that might once have belonged to celebrities is now widely available to the middle class; and it is the goal of the photojournalistic wedding photographer to make the everyday bride look as if she had just stepped off the red carpet at a movie premiere.

The Brights were accomplished in their genre, and their Web site showcased a catalog of images, in moody black and white and in color, that looked as if they belonged on the pages of a glossy magazine, showing couples captured in moments of unstaged but scrupulously edited intimacy. On the occasion I joined the Brights they had been engaged to shoot the entire wedding day, from the preceremony preparations to the reception at a local hotel, and so, in the late morning, while Stefan went off to join the groom and his party, I joined Linda at the bride's home. It was a modest suburban house with three bedrooms, a dining room in which the fancy crystal was arrayed in a glass cabinet, and two separate rooms for watching TV. When we got there it was already filled with excited women: In the basement, the bridesmaids were having their makeup and hair done, curling-iron tendrils falling around each girl's face; while the bride's mother was fretfully removing half the eye-liner and eyeshadow that had just been applied in a thickness suitable for the stage. The bride's father was wandering around the house in a pair of tuxedo pants that were too big around the waist, having failed to check the fit before that morning.

Linda moved carefully from room to room, snapping shots of the assembling family members, but also of the omnipresent bridal paraphernalia: in the living room, a box from the florist containing the bride's bouquet; in a bedroom, a lace-up corset, a pair of stockings, and a thong, laid out on the bed as if readied for a shoot for a lingerie catalog. When the bride went into her parents' bedroom to put on her gown, Linda followed for what are known in the business as "boudoir shots." "I didn't know they did them like that," said the bride's mother, anxiously, as Linda took a shot of the bride's gown being fastened under bared shoulder blades—one of those iconic moments sought out by every photojournalistic wedding photographer since the strapless wedding gown became the style of first resort among brides with the shoulder blades to carry it off. The bride, who had been calm until she put on her gown, started to look nervous. "I'm trying to take deep breaths," she said as her veil was affixed to her head and her bridesmaids gathered around, gasping at her transformation. "It makes you look really busty, dude," one said, appreciatively.

Everyone descended and climbed into cars for the journey to the church—the attendants in a limousine, the bride and her parents in a vintage Rolls-Royce—and as I waited in the hallway I noticed a wedding portrait of the bride's parents hanging on the wall. The couple had been married in 1979, only a couple of years after the Brights' own wedding, and the picture displayed the fashion signatures of the decade, with the bride in a white gown with blouson sleeves and the groom in an enormous bowtie in a shiny silver fabric. But their experience of the seventies could not have been more different from that of dwellers in a hippie ashram. Both were immigrants from Greece and had been raised in strict, traditional families; they married young and with little worldly experience.

The shot on the wall had none of the spontaneity that Linda had striven so hard all day to capture, nor did it depend upon the same cues—the bodice being fastened, the bouquets waiting to be called into service—with which Linda's pictures would prompt an emotional response from their viewers. But the picture nonetheless seemed to capture something essential about the couple as they stood on the brink of marriage, wide-eyed and a little awkward. This couple's daughter—who, as I looked at her parents picture, was being helped into the backseat of the Rolls, where Linda would almost certainly take a picture of her gazing thoughtfully out of the window, as she had done of countless brides before—would be born the following year.

The Greek parents' wedding portrait had less in common aesthetically with today's informal, romantic, and sexy wedding album—filled with shots so glamorous that they could serve as an advertising campaign for marriage—than it did with the kind of wedding pictures that were taken in the infancy of commercial photography, in the latter nineteenth century. These early pictures were sober studio portraits, often with the couple dressed in wedding finery, but sometimes not, and they would be taken either in the period before the ceremony or in the weeks or months afterward. Like the formal wedding portraits for which the Chinese workers at the Top Fashion factory might pose, even if they couldn't afford an actual wedding banquet, early wedding photographs sought to capture a rare image of the bride and groom as they appeared at the moment of such a significant transition in their lives; and the stiff awkwardness that such pictures typically reveal between newlyweds is not, one suspects, entirely due to the slow exposure times required for the picture's execution.

Formal portraits are still a standard part of a wedding photo album, but the purpose of wedding photography today is not to preserve for posterity a documentary image of the individuals who are getting married. (They, most likely, have already been photographed endlessly since moments after their birth, and, with the advent of ultrasound imaging, even before it.) Rather, wedding photos today capture a couple's specific incarnation as bride and groom, and their arrival at the apogee of romance. The album of iconic moments that the wedding photographer supplies to the bride and groom serves as the couple's confirmation that their wedding was, after all the effort involved, correctly executed: that they looked the way a bride and groom are supposed to look; did the things they are supposed to do; and—or so it is implied—felt the way they are supposed to feel. Wedding photographs do not so much portray the bride as she is, but as she would like to be: They are the documentary evidence of her self-transformation, of her prenuptial diet-and-exercise program and her acquisition of the sartorial savoir faire necessary to be able walk around in her gown without tripping. The groom—a lesser if still significant figure in a wedding album—appears as a far more dashing version of himself, dressed in clothes of unprecedented formality, and with fingernails at least freshly clipped if not subjected to a full manicure. It is this function of wedding photography that was drawn upon so effectively by JCPenney with its advertising campaign featuring LeAnn Rimes and Dean Sheremet—who, even though they were celebrities, persuasively approximated ordinary people who were done up to the nines and were the beneficiaries of a particularly talented photographer.

As I watched Linda Bright at work, I was also reminded of another function of the wedding album: as a means of capturing images of the material production upon which so much thought, time, and money have been expended. The wedding album serves as a riposte to the disquieted murmurings a wedding can generate among family, friends, and the couple themselves—all this, just for one day?—by ensuring that the spun-sugar flowers on the wedding cake and the silk grosgrain ribbons wrapped around the bouquets' stems are preserved not just in memory, but upon archival-grade photographic paper.

A good set of wedding photographs can be called upon to justify all the expense that preceded them; and the anticipation of acquiring a good set of photographs can also encourage that expense in the first place. When one contributor to the Disneymooner message boards wrote that she was wavering over whether to shell out for a character appearance at her reception, another contributor wrote, "Everyone understands Mickey & Minnie all dressed up, plus you get great photo ops for both your photographer & videographer to capture." The Knot bride who downscaled to chicken for the sake of her photo budget was able to do so because the degree of tastiness of a wedding meal can be sacrificed without compromising the event's pictorial record, even if doing so results in the odd disgruntled uncle.

There is one wedding expense that no bride wants memorialized in her wedding photographs, however: that of her wedding videographer. One of the consequences of the importance placed upon the visual documentation of a wedding day is that there can be so many more documentarians to deal with: The presence of a two-person camera team as well as a two-person videography team is not uncommon, to say nothing of the amateur photographers and videographers among the guests. The effort on the part of photographers and videographers to document a wedding without endlessly getting into one another's frame or otherwise having their technical capacities hampered can turn into a comedy of errors: "I must admit that my heart sinks when I hear there will be a professional videographer at a wedding I am going to shoot," one photographer wrote on an online forum. "When a videographer flips on the 20,000 watt, highly directional spotlight (with its telltale BOOOOF sound effect), the ambient mood lighting goes to hell in a hand basket."

Since 1995, videographers have been represented by a group called the Wedding & Event Videographers Association International, or WEVA. I first came across WEVA at the Business of Brides conference, in Kansas City, where I saw a presentation by Steve Wernick, who was then the association's public-relations chief. He showed a DVD of the kind of wedding videos members might be expected to produce: a bride and groom whose wedding had taken place during an unexpected snowstorm, tramping through the falling flakes and mounting drifts; a bride and groom pictured through a waterfall, out of focus behind the sparkling cascade; a groom picking up his bride, three times his size in her enormous gown, and carrying her along a picturesque country path, as if she were a Victorian lady in the midst of a fainting fit. Also included were interviews with satisfied clients. One mother of the bride said, "If I had paid twice what I paid for it, I would have felt I got my money's worth," while a bride said, "The video was the one thing we thought we could live without, but it would have been the biggest mistake we ever made." One hefty, florid bride, who was pictured dancing with her appealingly geeky husband, told the interviewer, "I believe it will help my marriage in times to come when things get hard. I can watch us adore each other, and I can remember how that felt, and what that was like."

The images on the DVD were affecting, and were further enhanced by the string quartet soundtrack and the well-chosen use of the slow dissolve. After the show was over, Wernick said, "When I show the film to anyone other than a videographer, I make sure to point out where the bride says, 'I believe it will help my marriage.' I can't believe there's a stronger message to a bride than that. And when I play it to videographers, I emphasize what the mother said, 'I would have paid twice as much.'"

That line drew chuckles from the audience, but I was struck by the evident conviction of the bride that her wedding video might have talismanic properties—that it was not just a record of her nuptial happiness, but might provide a guarantee of its endurance, or at least an insurance against its dwindling. It was certainly a powerful marketing message for WEVA, whose members devote a lot of their time to figuring out how to make a convincing case for the value of the service they provide to brides who may be otherwise preoccupied with selecting and paying for the material production of the wedding itself. "You have to get them initially, before they spend $3,000 on napkins," is how one article in *Wedding & Event Videography*, the association's magazine, put it.

On members-only message boards on WEVA's Web site, videographers exchange tips on how to be more relevant than napkins. In one thread, members discussed the best strategy for marketing a wedding video as "the most valuable heirloom your bride will keep from her wedding day." "I usually cite a moment when I walked in and found my 3 year old pulling out all of the guts of a VHS . . . which helps lead me into talking about how her (the bride's) future children will love watching and hearing every sight and sound from her wedding day," wrote one contributor. Such heart-tugging pitches do not, however, work with every bride and groom. "I always advertise that 'your production will become an heirloom that will be treasured in the future,'" another correspondent wrote. "However I'm not sure that most young couples even think they'll ever get old, let alone plan for it." Another correspondent questioned whether videographers should, in good faith, pitch their products as valuable heirlooms at all, given the current trends in wedding video production. "Seems that the eye-candy we sell in the form of short videos with a lot of fast cuts, filters, effects and so forth is not very useful as historical data," he wrote. "You want to see 'grandma,' and how she looked and behaved, not how grandma looked in slow motion with her veil floating in the wind, in sepia, changing to purple."

The videographer's challenge is more complex than that of Barbara Barrett at the Bridal Mall, who might struggle with the economics of running a bridal store in a competitive marketplace but at least can be assured that almost every bride will want to wear a big white gown in the first place. It is different, too, from that of Beverly Clark, whose traditionalesque wedding products—the ring cushions and flower-girl baskets—are familiar bridal tokens, even if they aren't to every bride's taste.

Videographers, on the other hand, have to persuade potential clients of the value of something that is transparently far from being essential to the wedding's execution; and to do this, an emotional appeal must be made to the bride that differs in slight but critical ways from the appeals offered by the suppliers of other bridal goods. The DVD that I saw at the Business of Brides conference, with its snippets of real-life wedding videos, consisted of images of joy attained; but its intended use as a marketing tool was to inspire in the bride-to-be the fear that she would be making a grave error, forever to be regretted, if she failed to acquire a similar record of her own happiness.

From the perspective of WEVA members, the bride must be persuaded that without video her wedding day will, quite literally, be lost to her. "Professional videography saves and protects life's most precious and beautiful moments—as they actually happened," reads the Brides Guide on the WEVA Web site. "You have only one chance to be sure your wedding day is professionally captured . . . just one chance to be sure all of the emotions, the love and laughter are preserved for you to share again and again." The cliché that insists a wedding day is the happiest of a woman's life—a cliché that has been in currency since at least the Victorian era—is here modified by an alarming addendum: that without a visual record, that fleeting peak of happiness might as well never have been attained. The promise of ultimate joy is bundled together with the threat of irretrievable loss.

Although the marketing of wedding videos often depends upon striking this elegiac note, sorrow is not the dominant mood at the WEVA annual conference in Las Vegas, which is regarded within the wedding industry as one of the more fun events on the calendar. Unlike most wedding-related services, the videography business is dominated by men, which made for a distinctive vibe at the WEVA-ganza, a party in an enormous ballroom at the Bally's hotel that kicked things off the year I attended. The dress code seemed to consist of Hawaiian shirts worn loose over pants, or polo shirts worn loose over pants, or any other kind of shirt worn loose over pants. There were many more men with grizzled ponytails than are found in a typical cross-section of the population, and they were wandering around happily, holding bottles of beer and plates piled high with the offerings from the buffet: tortellini with Alfredo sauce, penne with tomato sauce, and other foodstuffs of the sort that make you want to wear your shirt loose over your pants.

Many wedding industry events are styled to emulate the celebrations upon which the business depends, like the fancy black-tie reception at the Field Museum in Chicago for the DEBI Awards, or the small, elegant luncheon—a wedding breakfast without the bride—that had been held in a rooftop restaurant for members of the Association of Bridal Consultants in Kansas City. The WEVA-ganza was more like one of those wedding receptions at which the bride's aunt gets looped on champagne and dances in stocking-clad feet to "We Are Family," the groomsmen perform an impromptu break-dancing competition, and the bride's enactment of the arm movements to "Y.M.C.A." is so vigorous that her strapless dress ends up sinking two or three crucial inches down her bust. The tables had balloons for centerpieces, and the DJ was playing wedding-reception favorites like "Celebration" and "Love Shack" and "Macarena." The assembled videographers, with or without wives and children who had come along for the week of fun, were out on the dance floor, one twisting as if he were trying to get gum off the bottom of his shoe, someone else cavorting in the dancers' midst wearing a huge bobble-head mask of Sammy Davis, Jr. They all looked as if they were having the time of their lives.

The purpose of the WEVA-ganza was the handing out of honors, of which there were a seemingly interminable number. There were gold, silver, and bronze awards for all aspects of wedding videos, from Wedding Highlights Production to Short-Form Wedding Production; as well as countless honorable mentions, so that it seemed that in WEVA, as in kids' baseball, nobody who participates goes home without a trophy at the end of the season. The prizewinning videos were overloaded with special effects—puffy clouds scudding across a blue sky behind a couple in postceremonial embrace; shots displayed at MTV speed of gowns and cakes and flowers and favors. Humor as well as sentimentality was the order of the day, and the videos were designed to appeal to male just as much as female viewers. The video that won the Wedding Pre-Ceremony Production award showed a groom jumping on a bed in his bare feet, while the winner of the bronze award for Wedding Post-Ceremony Production showed a groom saying, "In ten years I want to be with Jeannie. In twenty years I want to be with Jeannie. In fifty years I just want to be alive." "Creativity is what we want at all levels," said Roy Chapman, the association's president, who was greeted when he took to the stage with cheers and loud, seal-like barks of approval.

The next day, I wandered from one lecture room to another, picking up technical and marketing tips. There was a class for non-Jewish videographers on how to film Jewish weddings ("Never ever, never ever, *never ever* refer to a synagogue as a 'church'") and another on how to incorporate styles of filming derived from reality TV to the wedding video. There was even a seminar called "Business Everlasting," in which a lecturer explained how lucrative it could be to expand beyond wedding videos into memorial videos to be shown at funerals. ("This specialized niche of professional video has no off-season," the conference's brochure noted.) In one well-attended lecture,

John Goolsby, a videographer from Riverside, California, and the author of a self-published book called *The Business of Wedding and Special Event Videography*, advised his listeners to double their prices when they got home from the conference, plain and simple. He explained how, years ago, he had added a $1,750 package to his list—about a one-thousand-dollar premium over his next highest price—only to get a phone call soon after from a father of a bride-to-be requesting his top package, no questions asked. "I was blind to the fact that people want the best for their children," Goolsby told his audience.

In another class, Maureen Bacon, a videographer from Westminster, Colorado, suggested that a good wedding video should be much more than a straightforward record—with the camera set on a tripod in the rear of a church—and called for the videographer's active intervention in the course of the day's events, like that of a director shooting a drama. Bacon explained that she informed her couples in a prewedding meeting that she would require them for ten minutes immediately after the ceremony, so that, rather than standing at the front of the church greeting their guests, they could go through an instant reenactment of the ceremony highlights. "I get close-ups of the ring exchange and the lighting of the Unity Candle, and I get them to do the first kiss again," Bacon said, explaining that she would edit those details seamlessly into the ceremony footage without a telltale change in lighting, so viewers would not be able to tell that the first kiss was, in fact, the second kiss.

Bacon also recommended formulating a shooting plan with the couple a month prior to the wedding to secure their cooperation for the "money shots" (the term is one from the porn industry, a reference which Bacon did not explain): not just the romantic, reenacted first kiss, but comic shots that gave what Bacon described as "emotional balance" to the video. Bacon's standard comic shots include the "gift steal," in which one of the groomsmen scans the pile of wedding gifts when no one is looking—apart, of course, from the cameraperson. "That's a nice surprise for the bride and groom when they see the video afterward," Bacon said. Another of Bacon's favorite sequences was the "runaway" shot, in which the groom is taped attempting to make a final escape from the wedding moments before arriving at the altar, only to be restrained by his groomsmen.

Scenes of larceny and attempted desertion are not, typically, understood as standard romantic tropes. (In fact, they hearken back to the antique practice, now largely in abeyance, of family and friends treating a wedding day as an opportunity for often bawdy prank-pulling at the expense of the bride and groom. Today's garter toss is one of the few remaining remnants of this practice of sometimes violent bridal mockery.) But Maureen Bacon's talk demonstrated that what a videographer is attempting to do is to construct a narrative for the wedding day—a narrative that, while it might have elements of low comedy, is fundamentally a story of elevated romance that is derived from models familiar from movies and television. A wedding day goes by in a proverbial flash: a year and a half of planning condensed into five or six hours of celebration; and what the wedding video provides is the opportunity for the bride and groom to revisit their wedding from the perspective of an observer rather than a participant, and to see things happening on camera— the ring-bearer's nose-wipe before walking down the aisle; the mother of the bride dabbing her eyes during the vow exchange—which are not theirs to see on the day itself. While the wedding photo album crystallizes the day into a series of iconic moments, the wedding video establishes a narrative of the day, in which the couple are literally actors in their own drama, enacting— and reenacting—crucial moments of the ceremony for the benefit of the camera, and for their own viewing pleasure later on.

Why is it so important for a bride and groom to secure a record of themselves getting married, rather than merely experiencing the event as it happens? And how have WEVA members persuaded couples that their experience of the wedding will be qualitatively enhanced by the ability to revisit it later with the help of their DVD players? (Not all can necessarily be thus convinced: One contributor to the WEVA message boards wrote of being unable to sell his services to a bride who said she "did not want video because it might cause her to remember the wedding differently than the way she wanted.") One way is to persuade potential clients that the term *memory* should be understood not to refer to an inward mental process, but to a tangible product that can, for a price, be acquired and saved in perpetuity. "Cherished memories from once-in-a-lifetime events have been lost forever because the event was not professionally videotaped" is how Roy Chapman, the WEVA chairman, expressed it in his association's magazine, as if memories were not the imagination's storing up of events but were precious documents, like legal papers or children's first drawings, that might be lost if insufficient care is taken of them.

The implications of this elision of memory with product—so advantageous to the professional videographer, whose livelihood depends upon marketing the intangible—were vividly demonstrated at the WEVA conference during a lecture by Michael Nelson of Remember When Videos in Salt Lake City, Utah. Nelson, a trim, dark-haired man, explained that he offered forty different wedding video products, from a Date video to a Courtship video to a Love Story video. It was his goal to sell each couple as many different products as possible—which is why, he said, he never marketed his post-wedding products before the wedding, on the reasoning that if he did so a bride and groom might choose to reserve part of their budget for their purchase, instead of spending money on prewedding products and remaining unable to resist the postwedding ones later. (One very successful postwedding product was the daddy-daughter dance video. "I sell this every time," he said. "I say, 'Get this for your father as a surprise, it is guaranteed to make him cry.' It is a great present for the dads, who put the money out for the wedding. It costs a hundred and fifty bucks, and takes me an hour, and Dad pays for his own present.") Sometimes, Nelson explained, he'd invent entirely new products, depending on what took place at the wedding. If the bride's sister, serving as a maid of honor, sang a song at the reception, he would create a video of the performance and sell it separately from the standard video. At one wedding Nelson filmed an unexpected prank of the groomsmen: They tackled the groom in an attempt to steal the keys to his car, which the groom tucked instead into the bride's bra, confidently telling the camera his car was safe. "Then the groomsmen went to break into his car and I filmed them trashing the car," Nelson said. Nelson's willingness to keep the camera rolling while witnessing an assault on the property of his employer did not, however, seem to be founded upon the documentary principle of letting events unfold without interference. "I got a whole extra product out of that," he said. "We tripled the price of that reception."

The important thing, Nelson stressed, was to ensure that the bride and groom did not think that just because they had hired a videographer to record their wedding, that meant that they could expect to see everything that unfolded at their wedding included in the basic video they had contracted to purchase. "That way they don't get mad afterward, and say, 'This isn't here, and this isn't here,'" he said. "I can say, 'Well, you didn't buy it.'" It struck me as quite an accomplishment that, having established the notion that memories can be materially preserved, saved, and owned, a videographer could also claim default ownership of them—rather like an explorer who alights upon an island, stakes his flag into the sand, and claims the territory for the Crown, without consulting the island's native inhabitants as to their feelings regarding unsought subjection to an alien monarch.

But what was most interesting about Nelson's presentation was the way in which video was being used not merely to capture the experience of the wedding; it was altering the experience of the wedding as it was unfolding. He explained how, rather then just showing up on the day with a camera, he offered products to be displayed at the celebration itself, using video screens set up around the reception facility to show a video history of the couple's romance, or a movie of the bride undergoing her wedding-day preparations that had actually been shot a few weeks earlier.

Video features such as these served as excellent promotional tools for Nelson's own business—"It would be difficult to find an audience more qualified for your products than at the event itself," he explained—but they did, he acknowledged, present his staff of shooters with a logistical problem. The novelty offered by his video displays was so great that guests, rather than talking or dancing, would start to congregate around the screen instead; and even the bride and groom might become transfixed by their own images. "At one wedding, we had one set up by the cake, but it was so popular that the bride and groom said, 'Can we move it over near us?'" he said. "The bride and groom wanted to sit next to it all night and watch themselves." The videographer who was tasked with shooting that wedding found himself with endless footage of people watching television—which is not the kind of memory the typical bride and groom expect to find preserved on a wedding video, even if it amounts to an accurate record of events.

The scene Nelson was describing was comic, if also more than a little horrifying: the ultimate image of the wedding day according to the more regrettable precepts of Bridezilla culture, as an exercise in self-regard so grandiose that it has collapsed in upon itself. Rather than turning outward to the community of friends and family who were present to witness their transformation into husband and wife, this couple turned inward, captivated by a sentimental narrative of their own love story in which they were enacting romantic scenarios made familiar by popular culture.

Intimate captivation is, of course, common to all lovers, even without the visual aid of a romantic video: Every couple—in the early phases of their love, at least—tend to exalt in their own private myth of origin. But it is a distinctly contemporary turn of events that the wedding day itself has become an opportunity for a ritualized enactment of that intimate privacy—the privacy of a nuzzling bride and groom captured by a photojournalistic wedding photographer, or by a videographer who has staged the nuzzling to take advantage of the best lighting opportunities—rather than being a moment at which the bride and groom step forward openly to take up their new place in the public world.

Perhaps Nelson's video-struck groom and bride were so absorbed in their own recorded images because, paradoxically, watching the video provided them with confirmation of the reality that they were making a significant transition into a new status as husband and wife. And that is another purpose of a wedding video: to reassure a couple that their wedding is an event of real significance beyond being the biggest, most expensive, most exciting, and most exhausting party of their lives. They were playing the role of bride and groom not to convince the wider public of the validity of their newly acquired social status, but to convince themselves.

There was no videographer at the wedding I attended with Stefan and Linda Bright, but at the reception after the ceremony, which took place at a local hotel, I caught up with Stefan at work. He ran around, orchestrating portraits of the bride and her family in the reception hall's lobby, while the guests who milled around during the cocktail hour visited the sushi station, the pasta bar, the ice sculpture, and the counter upon which were set three whole spit-roasted pigs, floral crowns on their heads and the disconcerting appearance of grins on their well-cooked jaws. I watched Stefan's technique for getting group shots that did not look stilted and uncomfortable: He arranged the bridesmaids and groomsmen in a standard wedding-album cluster, like a sports team posing with a trophy, then suddenly urged them all to lean in, so that he could capture the motion of groomsmen elbowing one another aside and bridesmaids tossing their hair back in laughter. When, having finished taking pictures of the wedding party, he told them they could disperse unless they were members of the family, in which case he would need them for other shots, one of the bridesmaids looked at him in puzzlement. "We're all family," she said.

In a state of affairs relatively unusual for a contemporary American wedding, particularly one whose participants have grown up close to a major urban center, this bride and groom, both members of a tight-knit Greek community, had known each other more or less all their lives. And while their experience was not quite as circumscribed as that of the bride's parents, the bride's background was quite different from that of the reader at whom *Brides* or *Modern Bride* is aimed, who is assumed to be quite a worldly creature before she is transformed by the bridal industry into a glamorous, otherworldly one.

This much Linda and I had learned earlier in the day, when we had spoken to the bride while she was still padding around her house in blue sweatpants and little white socks. Her family was quite strict, she explained: She had just turned twenty-four, but she still lived at home, and had only been permitted to go to college in Manhattan on the condition that she commute to classes. And though she had been dating her husband for years, their intimacy differed from that of many much less established couples. "I don't want to sound all virginal or anything, but this will be the first night that we will spend together in the same bed," the bride told us.

After Stefan had finished with the family shots, and the cocktail hour was over, everyone moved into the hotel's banquet hall, where nearly two dozen large round tables had been loaded with silverware and glassware and set with floral centerpieces and candles that looked to be in hazardous proximity. When the bride and groom were announced by the leader of a Greek wedding band and ducked under an archway formed by the arms of their young, gleeful wedding party, the guests—there must have been more than two hundred of them—erupted into joyful, approving roars. I sat in a corner, watching Stefan dart around with his camera until the traditional Greek music had started up and the dancing was well under way. He came and sat down next to me. "They'll be doing this for the next four hours," he said, gesturing to the dance floor, where everyone, young and old, had joined hands, moving in a deliberate circle with steps that all but several eager if clumsy toddlers knew so well as to be able to perform without thinking.

There was, Stefan implied, not much else for him to do: He and Linda had taken pictures of all the requisite iconic moments, and the photo album they provided to this couple would be as powerful and as handsome as the rest of their work. "The wedding is one day, and then you have your memories; and the memories start to fade, and then you have your pictures," was what the *Modern Bride* editor had said at the Wedding March on Madison; and I was sure that the couple would be thrilled with the Brights' depiction of their romance. But what I will remember of this wedding was not the cut of the bride's gown, or the color of their floral decorations, or even their clasping of each other's hands as they rushed into the reception. What I will remember is the electric excitement of the guests—those among them who were married recalling their own initiation into married life, those who were yet to be wed wondering when their turn would come—as the bride and groom were announced as man and wife, mere hours away from their first night together. And I will remember the sight of two middle-aged men belonging to the bride's father's generation, lost to the crowd that surrounded them as they danced together, slowly circling each other like a bull and a toreador, dipping and lunging in an elaborate, mysterious choreography.

Nine

The New Elopement

One evening in late spring, I walked on Aruba's Palm Beach, a stretch of white sand along which the island's resort hotels are clustered, and there I witnessed a curious nuptial spectacle. On the sand outside one hotel, under a palm tree strung with small lights, an arbor decked with greenery and white flowers had been erected. It was a breezy evening—as are all evenings in Aruba, thanks to the trade winds that perpetually rake the island—and the arbor had been firmly driven into the sand in order to prevent its being blown over. Nearby, a small round table had been set up, its white tablecloth securely anchored, the gold ribbons tied around the chair-backs fluttering violently. As I watched, a young couple emerged from the hotel, the bride wearing a long white gown with gauzy, drooping sleeves, like a tropical Maid Marian, the groom in khakis and white shirt. They took up their places beneath the arbor, and a minister in a suit began murmuring the wedding vows.

It would have been the picture of idyllic retreat had it not been for a steel-pan player and a guitarist who were perhaps fifty feet away, and who were at that moment striking up a wedding march to herald the arrival on the beach of another couple. Bride number two was wearing a strapless, sequined gown, while her groom was buttoned up in a dark suit. They approached their own minister by walking along an aisle formed by two rows of tiki torches and strewn with palm leaves.

Similar ceremonies are enacted all the way along Palm Beach most evenings in Aruba. Couples can make their vows in groves of tropical plantings at one hotel; before guests sitting on a dozen folding chairs set up on the beach at another. Bride after bride takes her place, some in lace-covered gowns and some in floaty white sundresses, their grooms in formal suits or light-weight pants. As each day declines into dusk, couples pose at the water's edge for their photographers, pictured in solitary embrace before the sun's red sinking beneath the earth's rim.

Aruba was the culmination of my journey through the American wedding industry, a journey which had taken me from the opulence of the luxury stores of Madison Avenue to the contrived Victoriana of Disney World's Wedding Pavilion, and from a bustling factory floor in one of China's new industrial boomtowns to a church with a dwindling congregation in an economically demoralized corner of rural Wisconsin. I went to Aruba because I wanted to find out how the machinery of the American wedding industry, with its claimed turnover of $161 billion a year, influenced economies well beyond America's borders. Americans spend more than $8 billion per year on honeymoons, the most popular destinations being Hawaii, Jamaica, and Mexico. But I decided to go to Aruba because the island presented an intriguing instance of a country that, upon realizing the opportunities presented by the American honeymoon market, had gone to unusual and single-minded lengths to persuade American brides and grooms of the enticements of its shores, including changing its marriage laws in order to improve its nuptial marketing odds. I wanted, too, to understand the allure of the tropical beachfront wedding—an innovation that has gripped the imaginations of increasing numbers of brides and grooms in the past decade, and the fulfillment of which has become a priority for a growing segment of the wedding industry, that catering to the so-called destination wedding. What was the appeal for a bride and groom of marrying on a far-flung sandy beach far from home and in many cases far from family and friends as well, willing castaways in formal dress?

The day after my walk on Palm Beach, I had lunch in an all-you-can-eat buffet restaurant in the atrium of the Renaissance hotel in downtown Oranjestad, Aruba's diminutive capital city, with Aida Perez, the founder of a wedding planning company called Aruba Weddings For You. Perez was quietly seething. Her company had orchestrated the wedding with the floral arbor the previous evening, and she was infuriated that the hotel's catering manager had permitted the steel-pan wedding, staged by a rival consultant, to go ahead in such close proximity to her own. "*I* do weddings there; that is *my* space," she told me. "I got the hotel to put the lights in the trees and to plant more palm trees." The catering manager must have double-booked the beach by accident, Perez said, and I had the distinct sense that such a thing would not be happening again.

Aida Perez, a bright, brittle woman of middle age, is in no small measure responsible for the fact there is an Aruban wedding industry at all. In the mid-nineties Perez, who had formerly worked in the marketing department of the Wyndham hotel, was asked by Aruba's then minister of tourism, Tico Croes, to present a report on possible niche markets that might be developed. On the recommendation of that report an island-wide program called One Cool Honeymoon was developed, whereby recently married couples were entitled to discounts at participating restaurants or hotels. But Perez thought that Aruba should go further. "I said, you should go into weddings," she told me. "I looked at what was going on in St. Lucia, Jamaica, the Bahamas, Barbados, anything I could get my hands on."

Aruba, which has a population of just seventy-one thousand, is part of the Kingdom of the Netherlands, and at the time of Perez's research, the country's laws were such that only Arubans, as well as residents of the nearby Netherlands Antilles and of the Netherlands itself, could get married there. Other Caribbean islands, Perez realized, had been positioned not just as a place for Americans to spend two weeks after a wedding but a place in which they might actually get married, with residency requirements limited in some cases to twenty-four hours and minimal paperwork necessary.

This, Perez thought, was the direction Aruba should take; but shortly after she made her recommendations to Croes, there was a change in government in Aruba and talk about revising the marriage law was shelved. Perez decided nonetheless that the market was ripe for weddings even if the law would not oblige, and in 1998 she founded Aruba Weddings For You, arranging beach weddings for tourists who did not care that the ceremony had no legal validity. "I was offering a beautiful wedding experience; however, you had to apply for your license at home," Perez explained.

Another change in government put the legislation back on the table; and beginning in January 2002, Aruba's marriage law was altered to permit the weddings of nonresidents. The impact upon Aruba's marriage statistics was immediate: In the first year 149 weddings of nonresidents took place on the island, of which 83 were weddings of American couples. By 2004 the number of weddings in which both parties were visitors to the island had reached 426. These are small numbers, but they amount to a considerable demographic shift: By 2004 one out of every three weddings conducted in Aruba was of nonresidents; and of these, nine out of ten were American couples. It seems very likely that within a few years Aruba will be marrying more Americans than it does its own citizens. (While foreign marriage is on the increase in

Aruba, local marriage is another story: A provision in the new law made it much easier for Arubans to divorce, and in the first year after the change there were seventy-six divorces for every one hundred marriages.)

Even now that the law has been changed, a beachside ceremony does not amount to a legal marriage: All Aruban marriages must be solemnized at Oranjestad's Town Hall, an attractive wooden building from 1920 that has a freshly painted white exterior and, inside, polished wooden floors, crystal sconces and acid green stained-glass windows. It is one of Oranjestad's most prized historical buildings, although it has a less than consistently distinguished history: Built as a doctor's residence, it later was turned into a Chinese restaurant and bar, and afterward lay derelict for many years, occupied by vagrants. The Aruban flag—next to which just-married couples pose for photographs—stands exactly where the Chinese restaurant's bathrooms were located.

The bureaucrat responsible for handling the wedding surge is Betto Christiaans, the island's registrar. Christiaans is a portly, affable man who has been a civil servant for more than thirty years and has married more than two thousand people, as well as registering all the island's births, deaths, and divorces. He is able to conduct weddings in Dutch, English, Papiamento, the local language, and a bit of French for the occasional Canadian, and his sole gesture toward nuptial formality is to button the collar of the short-sleeved shirt he typically wears and hastily put on a tie. Christiaans had mixed feelings about the island's wedding boom, he told me when I visited him at Town Hall. "For me, it is more work," he said. "Every week I have two or three couples, and last Saturday I had four couples. If you look at it from both sides, for the economy of Aruba it is good; but for me and my colleagues, we have more work to do." No raise in salary accompanied the expansion of responsibilities. "Nothing," he said. "I got nothing, nothing, nothing."

Many of his fellow Arubans were determined upon the changing of the law to get something, something, something, and the international hotel-chain corporations swiftly established dedicated wedding-planning staffs to deal with the escalating expectations of American brides. "I have one bride who wants a U.S. wedding transported to the beach," I was told by Michèle Osbourne, a wedding planner who specializes in working with the hotels to get paperwork through Betto Christiaans's office, and who was an original co-founder of Aruba Weddings For You with Aida Perez. "She wants bamboo, with palm fronds. She can have it, but it will be expensive. She wants to do a butterfly release. We have a butterfly farm here, but they cannot guarantee that they will be ready to fly for the wedding. I tell my clients, I will do whatever is possible, but we have limitations. This is a small island, and we don't have the resources of a large island. I can't provide you with pale pink linens with fuchsia napkins—no one here has pale pink linens with fuchsia napkins. She wants votive candles on her reception tables. I tell her it's difficult with the wind to keep a hurricane lamp lit here."

Aruba's repositioning as a paradisiacal wedding location has required a certain exercise of imagination by its tourism authorities, since it lacks the lush grandeur and tropical exoticism of other Caribbean islands. Aruba—which is just six miles wide by nineteen miles long and lies not far from the coast of Venezeula—has an arid climate and a harsh terrain. Its bleak windward coast is entirely uninhabited, hospitable only to squat cacti sprouting between yellow rocks and to the occasional gnarled divi-divi tree growing with an inbuilt bias away from the wind. The hotels all sit along the leeward coast, where water piped in from the island's desalination plant—the world's second largest—has produced an artificial climate: gardens planted with florid bougainvilleas, and white-sand beaches edged with palm trees that, not being native to Aruba, have been imported from other islands. For the visitor to Aruba, the experience of leaving the comforts of the hotel district feels a little like visiting the back lot of a Hollywood movie set and realizing that the illusion on the screen is created only thanks to endless yardage of electrical cable, lights sufficient to illuminate a baseball stadium, a rainmaking machine, and the tireless efforts of innumerable gaffers and grips, costume designers and caterers.

When I met Jorge Pesquera, the president of the Aruba Hotel and Tourism Association, he was quick to point out the island's advantages over its rivals, however. Tourists could safely walk the streets rather than being immured in hotels; and the weather was irreproachable, so long as one isn't utterly set on having votive candles. "I think it has to do with the comfort of an exotic but civilized place," Pesquera said. "It's a very romantic place, no matter how you look at it. Some people think it is totally flat. I differ. I think there are some interesting hills."

Aruba's wedding boom has encouraged the entrepreneurial aspirations of a number of rival wedding planners to Aida Perez; when I visited the island, two years after the law had changed, there were at least four established companies vying for business, and new ones were entering the field as well. Perez, who started the whole thing, insisted that she did not resent the competition, but she was nonetheless critical of those whose skills she thought inferior to her own. The tiki-torch and steel-pan wedding that had disturbed her own event, she told me with disdain the next day, was the work of an amateur. "I am leery of the torches because of the breeze—with a veil, there might be an accident," she told me. "And I would never have allowed my wedding to be out in the open like that, because the clients are going to be squinting. It's not just sand and water you need, but a bit of palm somewhere. It's taken a lot of practice."

Furthermore, she said, the timing of the other wedding had been off—the ceremony had started too late to ensure that the photography session afterward would occur when the sun was at its optimal level above the horizon. "I want my couple to get their sunset," Perez said sternly. "They have paid for that sunset."

·   ·   ·

Why does the castaway fantasy hold so strong for American wedding couples? Europeans who get married in Aruba get dressed up for the civil ceremony and tend to consider a beachside reenactment superfluous to requirements, I was told by Betto Christiaans, while Americans show up to Town Hall in shorts and save the ballgown for the sand. Sunset wedding portraits are so essential a part of the experience for Americans that if a couple gets married on the rare evening when the Aruban weather does not conform to expectations, they are likely to return the next evening, in bridal costume, to reshoot the portfolio.

In a way, I realized, the beachfront wedding took Colin Cowie's recommendation—that a wedding should be an expression of the couple's individuality, unhampered by the dictates of etiquette or the preferences of older generations—to a new extreme. The weddings that I saw take place on the beach in Aruba had none of the extravagant theatrics of Colin Cowie's productions and didn't even aspire to emulate them. But in placing the bride and groom in isolation at the water's edge, they emphasized their separation from the customs of the civilization, which, in fantasy at least, they had left behind for the duration of their wedding and honeymoon. (In reality, of course, civilization is close at hand just out of the camera's view, with swimmers taking the day's last dip, young people in sarongs and shorts sipping from glasses festooned with paper umbrellas, and diners tucking into lobster specials. The bridal photographs may later evoke solitude of the sort Robinson Crusoe experienced, but the reality has more in common with MTV Spring Break.)

Today's beachfront wedding and the honeymoon that follows it are understood to be an escape from the social world, a function that could not be more distant from the honeymoon's origin, in the eighteenth century, when brides and grooms would take a postnuptial "bridal tour" of the homes of relatives and friends. The contemporary idea of the honeymoon as romantic

retreat—one that is amply facilitated by the efforts of the tourist industry—
dates back to the middle of the twentieth century, when honeymoon-specific
resorts aimed at a generation of postwar newlyweds flourished. In the Poconos,
a celebrated honeymoon destination in the 1950s, hotels competed with one
another to advertise the most sensually enticing furnishings—a wall-to-wall
hexagonal bed, a king-sized bed flanked by marble columns—and bathrooms
primed for sybaritic indulgence. ("A flash of Pompeii splendor is reflected
in the sunken tub! Submit to it!" commanded one alarmingly peremptory
advertisement.)

A postnuptial trip in the mid-twentieth century provided a first opportunity for what a sociology paper from 1964 by R. Rapoport and R. N. Rapoport
soberly characterized as "developing a competence to participate in an appropriate sexual relationship . . . (and) developing competence to live in
close association with the marital partner." This was so much the purpose
of a honeymoon in the fifties that in one sociological study about honeymoons, conducted in 1958, 87 percent of the sexually uninitiated took such a
trip, while only 47 percent of those who had not saved themselves for marriage thought a honeymoon worth the effort. In a fascinating account of
women's recollections of their honeymoons that was published in 1947 in
the journal *Marriage and Family Living*, it was reported that three-quarters of
the sample considered "adjusting sexually" to be either the first or the second most significant difficulty that arose during the trip in question. (Among
the other causes of difficulty listed was, in the case of one respondent, "de-
testing the man," a condition not likely to improve even after practice.)

Today's couples have most likely already developed the first of the
Rapoports' competences, at least; while the wiser among them will also have
recognized that the latter competence takes a lifetime to achieve and is not
likely to be acquired during a fortnight at the beach. Sex is hardly the primary
focus of the contemporary honeymoon, although there is currently a fashion

for a period of prenuptial chastity among couples for whom the marital bed is likely to provide no immediate surprises. (In one discussion on The Knot, several brides suggested that one week's abstinence should provide an adequate wedding night frisson, which suggests a rate of premarital intimacy such as could hardly be improved upon even if that were the honeymoon's sole pursuit.) Rather, the honeymoon is understood to be an opportunity for recovering from the physical, emotional, interpersonal, and financial stresses of planning and executing a modern wedding—of which the honeymoon is a crucial, costly, and often otherwise-fraught component. The honeymoon is a honeymoon from the wedding itself.

The destination wedding of the sort that Aruba offers can certainly provide a bride and groom with an escape from the various pressures of putting on a wedding at home; and the increasing legitimacy of the notion of fleeing to the beach to get married is a boon to couples whose budgets or whose family dynamics—including but not limited to a set of divorced parents who can't stand each other—preclude more conventional nuptial events. But the destination wedding is also a boon to the tourist industry, which is well aware that honeymooning couples stay away from home more than twice as long as ordinary vacationers do, and are more likely to spend their money on luxurious additional services. As part of its efforts to court the destination wedding market, the Aruba Hotel and Tourism Association established an online island bridal registry whereby couples can register for products and services in lieu of more conventional wedding gifts. Extravagance and indulgence is the hallmark of the list, which features gourmet dining opportunities and spa treatments, including, at one spa, a treatment that doubles as a gourmet dining opportunity: a couples' massage with chocolate-scented oil, a chocolate bath, and what the brochure characterizes as a "soothing chocolate wrap."

With the honeymoon no longer functioning as a means of cementing new extended family ties or as a crash course in sexual intimacy, such diversions, often marketed explicitly as "once-in-a-lifetime" experiences, serve to reaffirm the momentousness of the commitment of marriage—which the wedding industry at large has already marketed to brides and grooms as the ultimate once-in-a-lifetime experience. Having drawn Americans to its shores, Aruba needs to keep them entertained once they are there; and, with a limit to the pleasures offered by its harsh natural terrain and its unprepossessing capital city, it is necessary to invent pleasures appropriate to the distinctiveness of the occasion. (As one article in the trade magazine *Travel Weekly* warned its travel agent readership, "The biggest pitfall for honeymooners is going to a resort and ending up bored.") A chocolate-based spa treatment may strike some as a sticky category mistake, but its availability as a honeymooners' diversion makes perfect sense. Its novelty promises today's newlyweds that there remains at least one pleasure of the flesh that can still be theirs to experience for the first time, and experience together.

"I call it the new elopement," Richard Markel, the director of the Association for Wedding Professionals International told me as we rode in a golf cart from one end to the other of the Half Moon, a resort just outside of Montego Bay in Jamaica, where the association was holding its annual meeting. Markel, who is based in Sacramento, where he runs bridal fairs as well as the association, spoke like a surfer dude—on the phone before the conference he had told me that it was going to be totally awesome, and that he was stoked to be organizing it—but he looked rather like a 1930s vaudevillian who'd hit late middle age, with a clipped mustache and hair tinted dark brown with a hint of aubergine.

The international professionalism of the Association for Wedding Professionals International left quite a lot to be desired, it turned out—the keynote speaker arrived a day late after failing to acquire a passport in time for his departure—but among those participants who did manage to get to Jamaica on time, there was plenty of talk about the new elopement. "Don't underestimate the amount of money that people are willing to spend for an amazing trip," Lisa Light, a wedding planner specializing in destination weddings, said in her presentation, her words echoing those of Antonia van der Meer, the editor in chief of *Modern Bride*, who spoke about the Echo Boom in Kansas City. "People who are in the age group that is getting married are going to one wedding after another," Light said. "A lot of these couples are the children of baby boomers who have made a lot of money, are adventurous in spirit, and have traveled a lot. So when it comes to the wedding, which is supposed to be the most amazing day of your life, it's kind of hard to top when you've had the kind of life they've had."

What Richard Markel might refer to as the old elopement was a resort for the romantic or the hurried: In nineteenth-century novels, the women who elope are those who resist the default expectation that their husbands will be chosen on grounds of economic prudence rather than at the pressing whim of the rushing of blood. (Elopement was also a resort for those already compromised by rushing blood, who wished to provide legal parentage for their unborn but imminently anticipated offspring.) The practice was firmly established in England in the eighteenth century, and was a means by which a couple might evade the reading in church of the banns—or announcement of the impending marriage—for three weeks prior to the event, and therefore avoid acquiring prior parental approval for the match. Over the Scottish border the same rules did not apply, which is why Gretna Green was the wedding resort of choice for absconding brides and grooms, who hoped that once the bride's honor was irredeemably compromised, her family would have no choice but to come around to the match, and would do nothing so unkind as to cut her off socially or financially. In America, where marriage licenses are issued by individual states, elopement came to mean running away to get married in a state that did not require a waiting period between the license being issued and the marriage being performed.

But the "new elopement" has come to mean something else entirely. Elopements are often no longer conducted in secret: Parents and other family and friends are in many instances invited along, with the bride and groom sometimes earning free accommodation according to the amount of business they drive their hotel's way. The authority whose control is being circumvented in a new elopement is that of the wedding industry itself, and the pressures exercised by Bridezilla culture. "I am so overwhelmed, I'm going to elope," wrote a bride on The Knot. "Here's what I haven't done: gotten a dress, food, photographer, centerpieces, decorations, etc, etc, etc. I'm a full-time college student and I work like crazy and I feel like as soon as I get one thing crossed off the list five more get added."

But while the new elopement might provide couples with a way to avoid the stress and expense that getting married seems to demand of them, it does not really amount to an escape from the wedding industry at all. While in Jamaica I visited one hotel, the Sandals Royal Caribbean, which is a veritable wedding factory. The Royal Caribbean is part of the Sandals chain, which was started in Montego Bay more than a quarter of a century ago by Gordon "Butch" Stewart, one of the best-known businessmen in Jamaica. Sandals is a dominant brand in the Caribbean's honeymoon marketplace, with hotels not just in Jamaica but also in Antigua, St. Lucia, and the Bahamas. The company offers mass-market resort escapism, with all-inclusive prices for food and liquor (the waiters and other staff at Sandals resorts wear buttons that read NO TIPS) and recreational options—scuba diving lessons, spa treatments—that provide an occasional respite from the poolside indolence that is a Sandals resort's primary appeal.

Sandals was an early innovator in the destination wedding market, trademarking the term *WeddingMoon* in the mid-nineties when the idea of an American couple traveling to a tropical beach to get married was still a relative novelty. In more recent years the chain has established co-ventures with other wedding-industry players: Beverly Clark produces a range of wedding accessories decorated with shells specifically for Sandals resorts, and Preston Bailey, the wedding designer who created the winter-wonderland extravaganza for Joan Rivers's daughter, Melissa, was brought on as a designer of higher-end wedding packages for couples who want more than the simple productions that are Sandals's stock-in-trade. By the time I visited Montego Bay, Sandals was hosting twelve thousand weddings per year, and of these an average of five, and sometimes as many as ten, were taking place daily at the Sandals Royal Caribbean, one of three Sandals resorts in town.

I was greeted in the lobby of the Royal Caribbean by Patria Clarke, one of two full-time wedding planners, who took me on a tour of the hotel's attractions. Its design alludes to that of the Georgian plantation houses that lie in the Jamaican hills not far away, with landscaped gardens and airy terraces through which the tropical breezes course—though the Royal Caribbean has the additional features of a swim-up bar and a series of artificially scalloped beachlets. Guests snoozed in loungers that had been dragged into the shallow waters, their reveries occasionally interrupted by the roar of a low-flying 757 arriving or departing from Montego Bay's airport, which is practically next door to the hotel.

It was that most unlikely of places: a beach resort where there was absolutely no sense of flirtation in the air, no cruisy buzz, or risk of a random, ill-advised pickup; just sunburned guys and women with freshly woven cornrows wandering, two by two, from beach to pool to all-you-can-eat buffet to bar. Like all Sandals hotels, the Royal Caribbean is a couples-only resort. (Until 2004 Sandals did not permit same-sex couples; for the sake of public relations they have since been officially admitted but have yet to make much of an impact upon the chain's guest demographics.) In the hotel's gardens, Clarke and I passed a couple whose wedding had taken place the day before. The bride, in shorts and a T-shirt, padded a few paces behind her new husband in silence. Both looked shattered, as if they'd spent the night boarding up their hotel room windows in expectation of a hurricane.

"How's the honeymoon?" asked Clarke.

"Great," said the bride, listlessly. "We're a little tired today."

"Too much champagne," said Clarke, brightly.

The center of wedding operations at the Royal Caribbean is an office just off the main lobby, where coordinators meet with couples the day before their ceremony. A basic Sandals wedding comes free with a stay of seven nights or more, and there is a limited menu of package options from which a couple can make selections. The morning I was there, Clarke's colleague Vanette Coleman was meeting with a couple from Oak Ridge, New Jersey, who were in their late twenties. He had a custom motorcycle painting business, and she was an OB-GYN nurse. "A friend came here on vacation who had had a big expensive wedding, and she said they wished they had done it here," the bride said. "It's simple, but nice and elegant."

Coleman was flipping through a ring-binder of photographs and making notes on a chart. Daisies or carnations were part of the basic wedding package. "You can upgrade to a thirty-five-dollar tropical bouquet, if you want, or it's fifty-five dollars for roses or orchids," she said. "And do you want ribbons?"

"I'll go without ribbons," said the bride.

"Do you want to go with the traditional wedding march or do you want instrumental music?" Coleman asked.

"What do you think?" the groom asked the bride.

"I think just the instrumental," the bride said. "It will take the pressure off."

"The day before we left to come here, I was so anxious I couldn't sleep," the groom said. "I drove twenty miles to the only twenty-four-hour deli around. Then last night when we got here I went to bed at eight o'clock, and now I'm ready for the rest of the week."

Two weddings were scheduled for the midafternoon that day, but the muggy skies and the local weather report were conspiring to deliver rain, and the ceremonies had hurriedly been pushed forward. The first bride, led by her tearful father, made her way through the hotel's garden and past a beachlet where the remains of a string of flowers that had been used for an earlier ceremony lay in a heart-shaped ring on the sand, lapped by the tide until it was no longer heart-shaped but kidney-shaped. A portable boom box had been plugged into one of the groundsmen's power outlets, and "I Can Be Your Hero, Baby," could be heard, quietly, beneath the sound of the waves, the CD skipping occasionally. The bride and her father walked along a short pier that led to a gazebo. Moored at a neighboring pier were several canoes whose Jamaican pilots were arguing loudly among themselves, and the wedding guests shushed them across the water.

The ceremony was performed by the Reverend Terrence Gordon, a local minister who conducts most of the weddings at the Royal Caribbean as well as at two other properties nearby, and who claimed to have married 10,270 couples over the previous twenty-five years. After the vows had been exchanged, the wedding party hurried back from the gazebo to a corner of the garden, where a table had been set up with a plate of hors d'oeuvres and a two-tiered cake. "I hope we can rush through these weddings," Clarke said as she looked up at the sky warily. The photographer hovered around the newlyweds and Coleman started issuing commands. "After three, look down and slice the cake—*one, two, three,*" she said, and the photographer snapped on three. The bottle of champagne was cracked and poured, and the groom made a toast, "To my beautiful wife, who brings me more happiness and peace than I ever thought I would have." Coleman told the guests—a handful of family members—to tap on their glasses with their forks. "They will kiss for as long as you tap," she said, and the couple kissed for a long moment.

"Okay, that's enough," said the bride's father.

"Cheeks together," said Clarke, and the photographer snapped. Clarke served slices of the top layer of cake to the guests, and then, discreetly, handed the bottom layer off to Coleman: It was artificial, and would serve for the next wedding, which was coming right up, on the beach.

Groom number two was wearing Teva sandals with his suit, and the bride was barefoot in a full white gown. (Couples can get married in modest beach-wear at Sandals—the bride can wear a bikini top but must cover up her lower half with a sarong or some such, while the groom must at least be in shorts and a tank top. Most, though, wear close to full bridal get-up.) They were get-ting married on the sand, and a brisk wind was whipping up. It was too breezy to lay down a ring of flowers, and the one left over from the earlier ceremony was now floating, sodden, in the water. "In the neighborhood behind us here, it's pouring," said Clarke, with another glance at the sky. Raindrops splattered on the best man's shirt. There was a flash of lightning overhead and the bride grimaced.

After the ceremony was over, the party hurried, in steadily increasing rain, to the aerobics room of the hotel's gym, where the table that had been set up for their planned garden reception had just been moved. The gym had a pleasant setting amid trees, with a high vaulted ceiling, parquet floors, and large windows; and only a couple of guests were working out, riding station-ary bikes while watching *South Park* on a TV monitor. The bride and groom posed—"After three, look down and slice the cake—*one, two, three*"—and the photographer snapped, taking care to exclude from the frame the brightly colored exercise balls pushed to the corner of the room and the heart-rate target chart pinned to the wall.

The efficient dispatch of so many brides and grooms depends upon making each wedding as much like the last one as possible, and production mistakes occur. That morning, Clarke handled the complaints of one couple who, upon watching their Sandals-produced wedding video in their room, discovered that it closed with a shot of another couple entirely. (The videographer, Clarke explained apologetically, had confused the two grooms, who both had short brown hair.) On Clarke's desk lay a vow-renewal certificate that had been prepared in advance of a ceremony; it announced that the couple "renewed thier vows" in ornate, misspelled calligraphy.

There is about one vow renewal for every six weddings at the Royal Caribbean, and to the wedding industry the phenomenon of vow renewal offers the very suggestive hope that the pool of available consumers—characterized to me by Gary Wright, the head of the National Bridal Service, as "the purest example of an inelastic market"—might turn out to be more flexible than expected. Hallmark introduced its first vow-renewal greeting card in 2001, and hotels have been particularly eager to embrace the practice. The celebrated Don Cesar hotel, in Saint Petersburg, Florida, managed to fill its off-season rooms with attendees at a mass vow renewal two years running, offering renewers a poolside ceremony with two hundred other couples as well as an optional relationship seminar conducted by a local marriage-counseling expert.

While at Sandals I saw the vow-renewal ceremony for which the misspelled certificate had been prepared: that of a couple from Philadelphia. I spoke with them before they underwent the ceremony. "We decided to renew our vows every five years, just to make sure everything is all right," the groom told me. He wore a silky white pajama outfit, while the bride wore a strapless white dress and was flushed with the sun.

As they went out to the beach, strains of Chic's "Le Freak" wafted over from the bar. The minister asked a nearby couple lying in the shallows to move away from the wedding site, and then murmured his way through the vows, pausing to push a lock of the bride's hair back behind her ear for the benefit of the photographer. The couple, having removed their wedding rings before the ceremony, slipped them back on to each other's fingers, looked at each other with deep tenderness, and kissed when the minister told them to. "Do it again!" their friends cried after the kiss, brandishing cameras.

I found the ceremony moving, even as the disco music from the bar offered unsought accompaniment, and even as I was aware of the wheels of the wedding industry grinding profitably with every gesture. Although the phenomenon of the vow-renewal ceremony may be an industry contrivance, the impulse on the part of the couple from Philadelphia to restate their commitment was genuine; and it was heartening to see a couple who already knew what marriage was emerge from the midst of theirs to vouch for its quotidian values.

But what I also saw on the faces of this husband and wife was the pleasure of enacting, once again, the parts of bride and groom, even as the ceremony had little of the meaning that has traditionally belonged to a wedding ceremony. It had no legal status; it was not a passage from one social position to another; it was not a joining of families. Instead, it was pure role-play.

I was reminded of a conversation I had at the Bridal Mall, the wedding-gown store in Connecticut, with a woman who was accompanying a cousin who was shopping for a gown. She'd been married for five years, but she told me that she hadn't had a wedding: Her parents had offered to pay for her to have a new kitchen installed in her house instead, and she had opted for the construction. "I thought, we can always renew our vows later," she told me. "And then, when we do, the kids can come as well." Hers was a practical perspective, but it also revealed an evolution in the way we think about weddings. The suggestion was that a wedding is, above all, a big party, one that might be delayed so that one's kids can have the fun of participating. This is quite a shift from the notion that a wedding is, above anything else, a party specifically celebrating the founding of a new family unit and the embrace of that unit within the larger social sphere, with progeny as an enticing future prospect rather than a realized fact requiring the hiring of babysitters, the purchase of flower-girl outfits, and the provision of an alternative menu of chicken nuggets and pizza.

The Sandals vow renewal provided a key to understanding the contemporary American wedding, too. The opportunity it offered the couple to affirm their commitment to each other was clear, and touching to witness. And the groom's conviction that the regular reenactment of the gestures of romance would aid the health of their marriage—like that of the bride on the WEVA promotional video who believed that repeat viewings of her wedding video would be salutary to hers—was sincere, even if the repertoire of gestures prescribed by Sandals, like those I had by now seen prescribed for brides and grooms throughout the wedding industry, seemed to me overwrought and at the same time impoverished.

But the vow-renewal ceremony also gave expression to yet another romance: the romance that takes place between the bride—and sometimes, the groom—and the wedding industry that supplies both the means to enact their roles and the scripts they end up following. This husband and wife were not just declaring the endurance of their love for each other; they were declaring their commitment to the American wedding, and to the American wedding industry that both serves it and generates it.

And this, I realized as I watched them on the sand, was the wedding package they were really buying into. It was the same wedding package sold to every American bride and groom by the American wedding industry, which provides not just the products and services for weddings, but the compelling fantasies upon which their use is grounded. This husband and wife were saying "I do" to the long white gown and the tiered cake and the wreaths of flowers—the trappings of the traditionalesque, bizarrely transferred in their case to the tropics. They were saying "I do" to the sentimental murmurings of a minister-for-hire, an official with whom they had no past and no future; "I do" to being, for a fleeting moment, the center of attention, and to having that moment ritually preserved by the flashing of cameras. They were saying

"I do" to their celebration as individuals whose own tastes and desires were paramount, trumping the practices of the past and the oversight of religious institutions and familial authorities; and "I do" to their consecration as a world unto themselves, there in romantic isolation at the water's edge, about to invent their future together. And they were saying "I do" to the wedding industry's own assumption of nuptial authority, administered through bridal magazines, bridal stores, department-store wedding registries, and all the other venues in which romance and commerce have become inextricably entwined.

And because of the wedding industry's ceaseless and ingenious innovation, there was, thanks to the phenomenon of vow renewal, now no limit to the number of times they could say "I do" to all of that. They could undergo this once-in-a-lifetime experience again, and again, and again, and again.

Epilogue

What is a wedding for? This sounds like a question to which there ought to be an obvious answer, but when I posed it to a group of soon-to-be brides and recently married women with whom I met near the outset of my research for this book—the question came perhaps an hour, and a bottle of wine or two, into a very lively conversation—the room fell momentarily silent, and then everyone broke into slightly embarrassed laughter.

The brides, whom I had recruited online for the discussion, had been describing with amused horror their own descent into wedding preoccupation, a condition not one of them—smart New Yorkers all—had ever imagined would be her fate.

"I thought, I am not going to get sucked in," one of them said. "But two hours after I got engaged, who was standing with twenty-five pounds of bridal magazines at CVS Pharmacy?"

"People talk about what kind of wedding you should have, that it should be individual," another bride added. "I want it to be individual, but it is so much work. It's like, 'What are your colors, what are your themes?' Sometimes I want to throw up, and sometimes I am, like, 'What *is* our color?'"

"I spent an entire month stressed about how much it would cost," another said. "I was not willing to sign anything, not willing to look at any dresses, just thinking, 'How many homeless people would this feed? Of how many countries does this exceed the gross domestic product?'"

What, then, was the point of expending all this time, effort, imagination, and money? What was the wedding for? The embarrassed laughter with which this question was greeted suggested that the question hadn't come up very much during these brides' own encounters with the wedding industry. They had become accustomed to thinking about the event in terms of floral decisions or styles of photography, with the larger purpose of the wedding a distraction from the more pressing questions of logistics; and they had hardly been encouraged to speculate more broadly upon the significance of a wedding by an industry that sought to ensure their total immersion in the business of brides. There was no column on the wedding-planning spread-sheet, no entry on the bridal checklist, for meaning.

Once asked, though, they were eloquent on the subject. The first said that she and her fiancé were both atheists, so they had talked about how to have a meaningful ceremony without it being about God. "For us it's a celebration of our love," she said. "It's about how excited we are, and how much we love New York. It is going to be this fun, wonderful time that is reflective of who we are, and about the joining of our families." The next said that her father-in-law had been disappointed by her plans' divergence from what he regarded as appropriate practice. "He said, 'A wedding is a family event, and this sounds like it is just a party for your friends,' and I remember thinking, that is *exactly* what we wanted, and asking myself how it could be both," she said.

Another chimed in. "I don't want to be living with my fiancé without being married," she said. "But I don't think it will change things, being married. In a way it is a formality, and in a way it is a party, and in a way it is a
chance to publicly acknowledge our families." Another who was Catholic and
was therefore required to go through Pre-Cana, the religious preparation
for marriage, told what had happened when, in one such session, the question had been asked, Why marry? "My hand shot up and I said, 'Well, it's
obvious—marriage is the joining together of two people as an economic institution designed to protect children,'" she said, drawing uproarious laughter from the brides gathered in my living room. "Some other girl in the class
said, 'Um, *love?*'"

All of these New York City brides wanted their weddings to have an emotional resonance, to be dignified and warm in proportionate degrees, and to
be distinct from the everyday. If the methods adopted by this small group
were not necessarily those that might appeal in more conservative parts of
the country (one, who was of Hungarian descent, said that she had become so
appalled by the prospect of shopping for and wearing a big white wedding
gown that she had toyed with the idea of dressing in an Indian sari instead),
their experience was different only in degree from that of millions of brides
across the country. All wanted their weddings to be significant; and all were
searching to identify the metal of that significance, seeking to burnish it
until it glowed. But there was no consensus on where that significance lay;
indeed, there were contradictions. A wedding was a celebration of family; it
was a celebration of self. It was a religious sacrament; it was an excuse for a
big party. It was an expression of personal taste; it was an enactment of tradition. What a wedding was for, it seemed, was up for grabs.

The one thing that did unify this group of brides, however, was that
each had encountered a wedding industry intent upon ensuring that her
experience of being a bride—whatever else it meant to her, culturally and

personally—amounted to a transformation into a new kind of consumer. Each had discovered that being a bride required an engagement with an industry that had interests very clearly at odds with her own and that depended for its economic health upon the perpetual spiraling upward of wedding-day expectations. Although these brides would have been dismayed to hear the terms in which they were, as a market segment, discussed by representatives of an industry that, in its public face at least, specialized in obsequiousness (a "drunken sailor," a "slam dunk," a "marketer's dream"), they nonetheless all had a shrewd understanding that their weddings were to the wedding industry a marketing opportunity above all. "It cracked me up when *Martha Stewart Weddings* sent me a subscription renewal," one said with a laugh. "I was like, I am getting married next year. I am not a repeat customer."

Each felt the pressure of Bridezilla culture all around her, even as she made efforts to avoid, for her own part, the behavior associated with that stereotype. "I was a bridesmaid for my very close friend a few years ago and I promised myself that I would never do what she did," one said. "Two years of planning, obsessing over every detail, whether the lining of the envelopes that she was sending the invitations out in matched the theme that matched the colors that matched the room that matched her dress." The pleasures of being a bride—in which each of these women took her full measure of delight—were admixed with a disillusioned sense that much of the role was being scripted by an authority no more elevated than the commercial interests of the suppliers of wedding goods and services. "A lot of brides make fun of the bridal industry at the same time as they get caught up in it," one bride said with a sigh. "We think we are better than that, but then we get caught up. I feel so betrayed by the wedding industry. They are feeding me, and I am suckered into it, but I love it. It is a real struggle."

Choosing between a cathedral-length or chapel-length veil for a church ceremony, or between Calphalon or All-Clad cookware for a registry list, is hardly the most vexing struggle in the world, but as I listened to these women, and later, as I made my way through the wedding industry that sought to cater to them, I realized that it would be a mistake to trivialize their preoccupations or to underestimate the depth of motivation that lay beneath them. They were, after all, not just brides—a temporary incarnation, albeit one that lasted sixteen long months—but young women whose experience of bridehood was only part of their navigation through a demanding and confusing contemporary culture. This was a culture that expected them to conform to stringent ideals of femininity, but also to assert their independence and individuality; it encouraged the most romantic idealizations of married love, but also made all too apparent love's insufficiency as a marital foundation; it venerated the idea of tradition, while voiding the practices of the past in its pursuit of the instantly disposable new.

Like Antonia van der Meer's Echo Boom brides, these young women enjoyed tremendous social freedom, having been raised to be the economic, political, and social equals of the men they were to marry; and, like the pregnant bride I saw married by Joyce Gioia with her mongrel spirituality, they had liberties, both before and after marriage, that would have been unimaginable to generations who preceded them. But their freedom from these strictures left them vulnerable, too, to the pressures and persuasions of an industry that sought to provide a substitute for those dwindling authorities, and, in so doing, hoped to win the immediate custom—and, in some cases, the lifelong consumer loyalties—of each of them.

In this respect the experience of the bride is only a particularly acute crystallization of the larger experience of all Americans, which is that of being immersed in a culture whose imperatives are derived more and more from the marketplace. And it is in this sense, too, that the American wedding should not be seen as a departure from the everyday—a "once-in-a-lifetime" moment, extraordinary and therefore permissibly extravagant—but as an expression of the most fundamental conditions of contemporary life. It may fall to each individual bride and groom to contemplate, and to figure out, the meaning of her or his own wedding, just as the New York brides so thoughtfully attempted to do as they sat in my living room, drinking wine and laughing over their own moments of nuptial beguilement. But when it comes to society at large, the American wedding—in all its excess and all its sentimentality—tells us what principles we are all married to.

About halfway through the research and writing of this book, I got married. It was not entirely a coincidence that my professional interests and my personal interests intersected in this manner—nothing of this sort ever is—but one did not arise directly out of the other, nor did one directly inform the other. I had decided weddings presented an intriguing subject for inquiry before I met the man I was to marry; and the directions in which my reporting for the book took me did not serve as covert research for my own nuptial plans. This book is not, in other words, a wedding memoir by other means; but neither was it written with the bride's questions—Would I do it this way? Should I do it this way?—entirely out of mind.

More than anything else, the discoveries I made about the workings of the wedding industry confirmed me in my long-held conviction that—in the event I ever was to marry—I wished to avoid its precepts as much as I possibly could. I had never, in any case, nurtured a desire to be a bride-by-the-book. I am not religious, and therefore had no institutional allegiance to a wedding site or belief that I needed religious sanction of my union. My parents, though happy to see me married, had hardly spent my adult life on tenterhooks while awaiting this blessed day—which, given that I was thirty-seven when I married and they were both into their seventies, was just as well. Meanwhile, it seemed to me to be something approaching an obscenity to blow on a single day's celebration of getting married money that could very usefully be put toward the considerable expenses of being married, which is to say the expenses of ordinary life.

Most important, though, I had no desire to place myself at the center of a nuptial production that seemed to have more to do with market-driven play-acting than it did the realities of historical practice, that bore little relevance to my own experience of romance, or of love, and that spoke little to my hopes for what marriage might mean. Marriage, it seemed to me, combined an awesome solemnity—an improbable vastness of commitment—with a playful, tender intimacy, the small sweetness of the everyday. To my secular sensibility, married love offered the promise of the transcendent within the day-to-day. Marriage, I thought, was like a medieval cathedral: striving in its structure toward sublimity, with its spire reaching for the heavens and the arch of its nave a prayer in stone, while, down at ground level, villagers huddled at the foot of massive columns and gossiped about the weather, their children larking underfoot. Whenever I tried to picture the modern American wedding, on the other hand, what I saw was an upscale shopping mall lined with brand-name boutiques offering luxurious, market-tested enticements to which I found myself immune.

A quick trip to the registry office might have been recommended by this situation; indeed, one of the most delightful weddings I have ever attended was that of friends who were married by a clerk in an office at New York's Municipal Building one morning before work, then walked with a handful of well-wishers halfway across the Brooklyn Bridge to toast the union with the city in full, spectacular view. But though I was averse to the conventional trappings of bridehood, acquiring a marriage license still seemed deserving of more ceremony than the acquisition of a driver's license; and while my friends' City Hall wedding was conducted in the spirit of an elopement—they were young, had met only a few months earlier, and did it swiftly in order to secure a green card—I wanted something different for myself. Like the brides I interviewed in New York, I wanted to marry meaningfully—which for me meant marrying with a consciousness of the momentousness of the occasion, but without the wedding industry's prescribed theatrics.

In the event, my husband and I were married on a Thursday afternoon at a New York City courthouse in front of a tiny handful of family and friends, the ceremony performed by a judge who was willing to officiate at the occasional wedding on personal recommendation. The ceremony was short but not perfunctory. We were dressed in everyday office clothes, and afterward we retired to the judge's chambers and drank champagne from plastic picnic flutes. A few days later we hosted a party for about seventy or eighty friends and family members at the house we already lived in. One friend did the catering, and another supplied the wine. Halfway through the evening someone clinked on a glass and there were toasts, too many of them. An R & B band my husband had recruited from a subway platform showed up to play for an hour or two, and there was dancing. We were lucky with the weather, and people sat out in the garden talking until two a.m. I wore an orange linen dress that was decorated with a floppy linen flower, the edges of its petals frayed.

Was this the "spin on tradition" of which Antonia van der Meer had spoken? Perhaps, in a way, it was. Our spin on tradition, though, amounted to an acknowledgment—a sad one, in a way, but an important one—that we were to a large extent without tradition when it came to getting married. Without the dictates of religious authority to follow, or the rituals of unwavering cultural practice to enact, we had no choice but to invent a wedding for ourselves. In just about every dimension of our lives we were at liberty from tradition's infringements, and grateful for it; but we were without tradition's anchors and consolations, too. This loss was lamentable, but inevitable; and we were far from alone in our experience of it. What made us different from so many others on the brink of marriage—what, perhaps, was the expression of our distinctiveness as a couple that Colin Cowie had said was the whole point of a wedding—was that we chose not to embrace the compensations readily provided by the wedding industry; which, given the commercial interests from which they arose, seemed to us to be no compensation at all.

During the three years that it took me to research and write this book—a period during which the wedding industry, according to its own figures, expanded by more than $40 billion annually—a passionate debate about the meaning of marriage was being conducted in legislatures, on op-ed pages, at workplaces, in schools, and in homes all over the country. What was being discussed was same-sex marriage: whether gay men and women should have the same rights to marry as heterosexual Americans do; or whether, conversely, marriage between same-sex partners was an abomination that should be swiftly and explicitly outlawed.

The debate, and its attendant civic action, was vivid and urgent, with victories and defeats for each side tumbling one after the other. The Massachusetts Supreme Judicial Court legalized gay marriage toward the end of 2003, and in the early months of the following year same-sex couples were wed in televised exhilaration in Boston and San Francisco and New Paltz, New York. By the end of the year, however, voters in eleven states had passed ballots that approved the banning of same-sex marriage, and disheartened Democrats were contending that the issue had cost their presidential candidate the election. As I write, in the summer of 2006, the question of whether marriage is "a sacred institution between a man and a woman," as President Bush has clumsily put it, or whether it consists of a set of civil rights to which gay men and women should be no less entitled than their straight peers has been under examination by legislatures from New York to Nebraska, while there are constitutional amendments restricting marriage to men and women on the ballot in six states in the forthcoming elections.

One predictable result of the optimistic flurry of gay-marriage activism that took place in 2003 and 2004 was the establishment of a new segment of the wedding industry, one catering specifically to gay couples. In the summer of 2004, I attended a gay-wedding expo in New York, one of several such trade fairs now held in cities around the country, where the booths were arranged in aisles named for Jason West and Gavin Newsom, the mayors of New Paltz and San Francisco, and where vendors advertised gay-friendly wedding-planning services and same-sex honeymoon alternatives ("I want to go to a place where I don't have to call my boyfriend my brother," read one advertisement on display from the Wyndham hotel chain). The increasing social acceptance of gay commitment ceremonies—the *New York Times* began including the unions of gay couples in its wedding pages in 2002, before gay marriage was legal in any state—meant that a market had presented itself, legal sanction or no. "It's hard for me to believe we can ignore the subject, and the disposable income," Udi Behr, a jewelry designer who was promoting a Love and Pride line of engagement and wedding rings, told an interviewer at *Crain's New York Business.*

Indeed, it was almost comical to witness the speed with which gay marriage was embraced as an economic opportunity, as well as to observe the fumblings of the established wedding industry when presented with the prospect of an unfamiliar new customer. "I think this is a huge untapped market," wrote one contributor to the message boards of a Web site for wedding-gown manufacturers and retailers. "However, retailers will need to be able to deal with the relationship in a professional manner. . . . When I started out with my same sex clients, I just flat out admitted that I knew nothing about their lifestyle and I needed to be informed of how they were to be referred to, who was the bride/groom, etc."

Even the most naked wedding-industry opportunism, though, could not diminish the profundity of the debate that was taking place—a debate that weighed the very purpose of marriage. Was it an economic and legal alliance above all else? An institution designed for the nurturing of children? God's intended program for his dearest creation? An oppressive patriarchal struc- ture that no self-respecting person, gay or otherwise, should want to enter into? It was striking to see that, during these wedding-boom years, some of the people who were thinking the hardest about what it meant to get married were those who were unable to marry the partner of their choice—or were, at least, unable to marry the partner of their choice without going to Canada or Massachusetts or the Netherlands to do so, and were uncertain of whether, when they got home, the documents certifying such a marriage would be any more valid than a Sandals-issued vow-renewal certificate.

This is not to suggest that all gay weddings or commitment ceremonies are performed in a spirit of perfectly accomplished self-examination; or that a gay wedding might not be the obsessed-over product of a wedding planner's lavish attentions just as much as a wedding of a man and a woman might be. (Indeed, a gay wedding ceremony might consist of the matrimonial unit- ing of two wedding planners, as was the case in September 2003, when David Tutera and Ryan Jurica, president and vice president, respectively, of David Tutera, Inc., a celebrity party-planning company, were joined in a civil cere- mony in Vermont, their union heralded in the wedding pages of the *New York Times*.) But participants in a same-sex wedding—the couple and their guests— are, perforce, obliged to think about the meaning of the undertaking in a way that is not demanded of their heterosexual peers.

Advocates of gay marriage argue that the more widespread the practice becomes, the more Americans will take it for granted. People who recoil from the abstract notion of men marrying men or women marrying women will feel differently, the argument goes, when they realize that those men and women are their neighbors, their fellow members of the PTA, their doctors, or their plumbers. But it occurred to me to wonder, as I listened to the gay-marriage debate unfold while making my way through wedding-gown stores, wedding-planning seminars, and beachside wedding ceremonies on Caribbean islands, what would happen if that formula were to be reversed. What would the American wedding look like if all Americans approached their weddings with the same consciousness as that demanded of gay couples? What if getting married was not simply something the average American—having found a suitable spouse—could do when he or she pleased, and in the manner he or she desired, but was a right that had been argued over and fought for? What if every wedding was a cherished victory won?

Acknowledgments

David Remnick, the editor of *The New Yorker*, published the piece that led to this book, permitted me extended leaves from the magazine to research and write it, and offered support, reassurance, and solidarity throughout. I am more grateful to him than I can say. Kathy Robbins, my agent, was wise in her counsel and dogged in her representation, and she has my enduring thanks. Ann Godoff, at the Penguin Press, lived up to her formidable reputation as a book-shaper and author-coaxer; I am grateful for her vision and her persistence.

Many people in the business of weddings were kind enough to speak with me and share their insights and experiences. To those who appear as characters in the book my debt is clear, and my thanks are due. I am particularly grateful to Nick Yeh for allowing me to accompany him to China and to the Top Fashion factory. Thanks go also to many others who spoke with me, including Preston Bailey, Barbara Barrett, Ron Ben-Israel, Jeffrey Best, Marcy

Blum, Millie Martini Bratten, Alan Dessy, Jim Duhe, Randy Friedman, Peter Grimes, Rebecca Grinnals, Nina Lawrence, David Liu, Susan McCullough, Carley Roney, Andrea Rotondo, Doris Nixon, Sylvia Weinstock, David Wood, and Gary Wright. I am deeply grateful to the many unnamed brides and grooms who allowed me to observe their weddings and who talked to me about their encounters with the wedding industry. Some of them appear in the book; many do not. Their stories informed my reporting at every turn.

Many other people provided invaluable assistance and information. William Crews, at the Centers for Disease Control and Prevention, patiently dug up relevant statistics. Robert Fuller, at Bradley University, offered guidance on the unchurched. Msgr. Anthony Sherman provided a Catholic perspective on the Unity Candle. Ken Blake at Middle Tennessee State University provided perspective upon that state's demographics. James Faris, Kay Parker Schweinfurth, Herb Stevens, and Johnson Dennison weighed in on the Apache Indian Prayer; thanks too to Robert Doyle at Canyon Records. Peter Hessler offered his insights on China. Bill and Mary Powell were generous hosts in Hebron. Kimberly Chase, Carrie Frank, Rebecca Sun, and Kersten Zhang all provided much-appreciated research assistance.

I am grateful to Liza Darton, Lindsay Whalen, Veronica Windholz, and Marlene Tungseth at the Penguin Press, as well as to Andrew G. Celli Jr. At the Robbins Office thanks go to Coralie Hunter, David Halpern, and Kate Rizzo. At *The New Yorker* thanks are due to Pam McCarthy, who makes everything run smoothly, and Bruce Diones, without whom, chaos. Peter Canby, in the fact-checking department, is indispensable, and my particular thanks go to Emily Richards and Marina Harss, the fact-checkers who worked on the article with which this book originated. Thanks too to Dorothy Wickenden, Henry Finder, Daniel Zalewski, and Ann Goldstein. To Susan Morrison, for many years my editor at the magazine, I am especially indebted; she read repeated drafts of this book, gave invaluable counsel and editorial suggestions, and has contributed enormously to making my writing life a very happy one.

Thanks also go to Nancy Novogrod at *Travel & Leisure* and George Kaloge-rakis, formerly thereof, who helped me get to China; and to Susan Kitten-plan, Linda Wells, and Andrew Wilkes at *Allure*, for their endorsement and forbearance.

In researching this book I relied upon the work of a number of scholars and writers who had taken weddings as their subject before I did and whose works I recommend to readers interested in finding out more about the history of the American wedding. The following books were particularly useful to me: *And the Bride Wore . . . : The Story of the White Wedding* by Ann Monsarrat; *Hands and Hearts: A History of Courtship in America* by Ellen K. Rothman; *Public Vows: A History of Marriage and the Nation* by Nancy F. Cott; *White Weddings: Romancing Heterosexuality in Popular Culture* by Chrys Ingraham; *Cinderella Dreams: The Allure of the Lavish Wedding* by Cele C. Otnes and Elizabeth H. Pleck; and *All Dressed in White: The Irresistible Rise of the American Wedding* by Carol McD. Wallace. Vicki Howard's book, *Brides, Inc: American Weddings and the Business of Tradition,* had not yet been published while I was writing this book, but the papers she published in academic journals were richly informative. Two journalistic treatments of the wedding industry, *For Richer, For Poorer,* by Kitty Hanson, which was published in 1967, and *The Eternal Bliss Machines,* by Marcia Seligson, which was published in 1973, were illuminating.

Many friends read this book, in part or in total, in earlier stages, and I am grateful for their suggestions. Thanks go to David Bornstein, Lauren Collins, Laura Kipnis, Edward Mendelson, Kate Sekules, Shari Spiegel, and Katherine Swett. Particular thanks are due to Scott Moyers, who came up with the title. Others supplied love and support without which this book could not have been written, and that is the least of it. I am especially grateful to Elizabeth Berger, Nick Denton, Paul Holdengräber, Abigail Gampel, Matt Greenfield, Emily Jackson, Molly Jong-Fast, Frederick Kaufman, Arabella Kurtz, and Christine Schwartz-Hartley. Barbara Wansbrough buoyed my spirits hugely while I was writing. Nina Roberts performed the ultimate mitzvah; she is in my heart. Anne LaFond has been an ally; she has my profound thanks. Thanks also go to Barbara Richards, whose broad kindness I depend upon.

My parents, Barbara and Brian Mead, have given me boundless love and encouragement, supporting me in every hope and ambition. Even at three thousand miles distance I feel the warmth of their embrace every day. My brother, Matthew Mead, and my sister-in-law, Julia Mead, have found time for me in their own too-busy lives, and I am deeply and fondly grateful to them. My parents-in-law, Martin and Marian Prochnik, have been kindness itself. James Jodha-Prochnik and Samoa Jodha, my brother- and sister-in-law, have been generous friends; Elizabeth Prochnik and Ethan Prochnik, my sister- and brother-in-law, have been instantly familial. Yona, Tzvi, and Zach Prochnik, my stepsons, have been a source of dinner-table enlivenment and all-around good humor; their inspired progress through life is a pleasure to witness.

My greatest debt is to my husband, George Prochnik, whose liveliness of spirit, quickness of wit, fortitude of character, and gentleness of soul have given me more joy and contentment than I ever imagined would be mine. Our meet and happy conversation sustains me, informs me, and delights me; without him, I know not what. The last word goes to my son, Rafael, whose arrival, while I was writing this book, changed it and changed me, and who every day provides me with one answer to the question of what a wedding is for.

Index